TECHNICAL REPORT #11

LANGUAGE LEARNING MOTIVATION: PATHWAYS TO THE NEW CENTURY

edited by REBECCA OXFORD

SECOND LANGUAGE TEACHING & CURRICULUM CENTER
University of Hawai'i at Mānoa

Second Printing 1999

Funds for the publication of this technical report were provided in part by a grant to the University of Hawai'i under the Language Resource Centers Program of the U.S. Department of Education.

ISBN 0–8248–1849–0

∞™ The paper used in this publication meets the minimum requirements of American National Standard for Information Sciences—Permanence of Paper for Printed Library Materials.

ANSI Z39.48–1984

Book design by Deborah Masterson

Distributed by
University of Hawai'i Press
Order Department
2840 Kolowalu Street
Honolulu, Hawai'i 96822

ABOUT THE NATIONAL FOREIGN LANGUAGE RESOURCE CENTER

THE SECOND LANGUAGE TEACHING AND CURRICULUM CENTER of the University of Hawai'i is a unit of the College of Languages, Linguistics, and Literature. Under a grant from the US Department of Education, the Center has since 1990 served as a National Foreign Language Resource Center (NFLRC). The general direction of the Resource Center is set by a national advisory board. The Center conducts research, develops materials, and trains language professionals with the goal of improving foreign language instruction in the United States. The Center publishes research reports and teaching materials; it also sponsors a summer intensive teacher training institute. For additional information about Center programs, write:

Dr. Richard Schmidt, Director
National Foreign Language Resource Center
East-West Road, Bldg. 1, Rm. 6A
University of Hawai'i
Honolulu, HI 96822

NFLRC ADVISORY BOARD

Kathleen Bardovi-Harlig
Center for English Language Teaching
Indiana University

John Clark
Defense Language Institute
Monterey, California

James Pusack
Project for International Communication Studies (PICS)
University of Iowa

Ronald Walton
National Foreign Language Center
Washington, D. C.

Representatives of other funded NFLRCs

CONTENTS

Chapter 1: New Pathways of Language Learning Motivation
Rebecca L. Oxford 1

Chapter 2: Foreign Language Motivation: Internal Structure and
External Connections
Richard Schmidt, Deena Boraie, & Omneya Kassabgy 9

Chapter 3: Moving Language Learning Motivation to a Larger Platform
for Theory and Practice
Zoltán Dörnyei 71

Chapter 4: An Exploration of Adult Language Learner Motivation,
Self-Efficacy, and Anxiety
Madeline Ehrman 81

Chapter 5: Not All Alike: Motivation and Learning Strategies among
Students of Japanese and Spanish in an Exploratory Study
Mayumi Okada, Rebecca L. Oxford, & Suzuna Abo 105

Chapter 6: Language Learning Motivation in a New Key
Rebecca L. Oxford & Jill Shearin 121

References 145

About the Authors 161

Rebecca L. Oxford
The University of Alabama

CHAPTER 1
NEW PATHWAYS OF
LANGUAGE LEARNING MOTIVATION

ABSTRACT

This chapter presents a short overview of the history of language learning motivation research, discusses current efforts to expand the theory of language learning motivation, and describes the contributions of each chapter of this book to that expansion. New pathways of language learning motivation are possible, according to this chapter. These take different forms, but all of them involve looking at "new" psychological variables and other factors that have not been included in the traditional social psychological theory of language learning motivation. In traversing these pathways, it is not necessary to jettison social psychology; instead, traditional theory has paved the road for current and future explorations.

INTRODUCTION

This book describes new routes of language learning motivation, avenues that will take us into the new century and the new millennium. These pathways have been ignored for many years. They are the ones that have been (as Schmidt, Boraie, and Kassabgy quote in Chapter 2) at the "neglected heart of language learning." For decades language teachers and researchers have been walking the well-known roads of social psychological theories of language learning, never venturing to explore the many possible intersecting pathways representing other branches of psychology. Without losing track of the well-traveled social psychological streets and without getting lost in any little byways, thickets, or weedbeds, it is time for us to look more widely at all the possible pathways in the realm of language learning motivation. For the sake of students worldwide, we cannot afford to restrict ourselves to a small set of motivational variables, especially when we know from research in other fields that motivation is an extraordinarily complex, multifaceted, and important construct.

This book chronicles a revolution in our thinking about what makes students want to learn languages and what causes them to put forth the effort to persist in that difficult adventure. To comprehend this revolution, led by outwardly mild-mannered researchers at institutions as far-flung as Hungary and Hawai'i and many places in between, it is necessary to understand something of the development of research on language learning motivation over the last thirty years.

Oxford, Rebecca L. (1996). New pathways of language learning motivation. In Rebecca Oxford (Ed.), *Language Learning Motivation: Pathways to the New Century*. (Technical Report #11) (pp. 1–8). Honolulu: University of Hawai'i, Second Language Teaching & Curriculum Center.

A BRIEF HISTORY

ON THE SOCIAL PSYCHOLOGICAL PATH

A single theory, in one form or another, has dominated the language learning motivation scene for about three decades. This social psychological theory was created and elaborated by Gardner and his colleagues (Gardner, 1985b, 1988; Gardner, Lalonde, Moorcroft, and Evers, 1985; Gardner and Lambert, 1959, 1973; Gardner and MacIntyre, 1991, 1993; Gardner and Tremblay, 1994b; Lambert, Gardner, Barik, and Tunstall, 1963). It is known as the Socio-Educational Model (Gardner, 1985b).

A desire for learning the language for the purpose of cultural/linguistic integration is found on all levels within this social psychological construct of language learning motivation. At the most specific or first level is found integrative orientation. An *orientation* (according to Gardner and Tremblay, 1994a) is a class of reasons for studying a language. Integrative orientation deals with the individual's desire for cultural or linguistic integration. Presumably other orientations are also possible here, though the integrative orientation is highlighted.

At the second, broader level are (1) integrativeness and (2) attitudes toward the L2 learning situation. These are considered precursors to motivation (Gardner and Tremblay, 1994a). *Integrativeness* refers to the integrative orientation mentioned above (i.e., integrative reasons for language learning), plus two attitudinal factors: general foreign language interest and attitudes toward the target community. *Attitudes toward the L2 learning situation* are comprised of evaluation of the teacher and evaluation of the course (Gardner and MacIntyre, 1993).

At the third level is the tripartite group consisting of: (1) effort (in some Gardner articles called motivational intensity), (2) desire to learn the language (called "valence" in Tremblay and Gardner, 1995), and (3) attitudes toward learning the language. These, taken together, are viewed as *motivation*.

Collapsing and somewhat simplifying these levels, Gardner (1985b) asserts that motivation is composed of four elements: a goal (orientation, found in the first and second levels), a desire to attain the goal (the third level), positive attitudes toward learning the language (the third level), and effortful behavior to that effect (the third level). This simplification leaves out some aspects of the second level: general foreign language interest, attitudes toward the target community, evaluation of the teacher, and evaluation of the course. Nevertheless, the simplification is a useful heuristic.

Gardner and Tremblay (1994a) state at this point in time that motivation is the central concept and that integrative motivation is not paramount in the Socio-Educational Model. Elsewhere Gardner states: "The source of the motivating impetus is relatively unimportant, provided that motivation is aroused" (1985b, p. 169). However, the Socio-Educational Model is imbued from top to bottom with integration in one form or another. Integration energizes the first three levels. Hence, it is understandable that discussions of this model use "the integrative motive" and "motivation" virtually interchangeably. Gardner and his colleagues have been questioned about their focus on integrative motivation as the primary or most important type of language learning motivation (Au, 1988; Crookes and Schmidt, 1991; Dörnyei, 1990a, 1994a; Ely, 1986b; Horwitz, 1990; Oller, 1981b; Oxford and Shearin, 1994).

However, integrative motivation at various levels is the central theme of their work, and time and again it has proven its importance in relation to language achievement, albeit within the particular social psychological research framework (see, e.g., Gardner, 1979, 1985b, 1988, 1992; Gardner and Lambert, 1959, 1972, 1975). According to much of the research, integratively motivated students capitalize on all practice opportunities, volunteer more answers in the classroom, are more precise in responses, and are more satisfied and rewarded for participation (Gardner, 1985b; Gliksman, Gardner and Smythe, 1982).

Integrative motivation as a construct is also supported by other sociolinguistic research. For example, in Speech Accommodation Theory (Giles and Byrne, 1982), the learners' degree of identification with the in-group (the group that speaks the target language and is therefore advantaged socially and communicatively) is directly related to the learners' success in acquiring the second language. Schumann's Acculturation Model (Schumann, 1978, 1986) seems to involve integrative motivation. Schumann (1978) suggested that second language acquisition is only one aspect of acculturation and that the degree of acculturation determines the level of second language acquisition. When an individual chooses to acculturate and experiences success, the motivation to learn the L2 increases, the person continues to try, and he or she progresses in L2 learning.

DOWN "INSTRUMENTAL LANE" WITH FOREIGN LANGUAGE LEARNERS

Gardner and group were criticized, perhaps a bit unfairly, for creating a somewhat false split between integrative and instrumental motivation (see, e.g., Dörnyei, 1994a; Oxford and Shearin, 1994). Integrative motivation has been described above. Instrumental motivation is motivation to learn the language for an instrumental (i.e., practical) purpose, such as getting a better job, earning more money, entering a better college or graduate school, and so on. Gardner and Tremblay (1994b) point out that only one study by the Gardner group in the last 34 years has considered instrumental motivation (Gardner and MacIntyre, 1991). They note that in 11 factor analytic or causal modeling studies in which Gardner was involved, with 21 different samples, all samples showed an *integrative motivation* factor and none displayed an *instrumental motivation* factor (though an *instrumental orientation* factor was found in three of the samples). Again, here is a distinction between the reasons (orientation) for learning a language versus the broader and more important motivation, of which the reasons are only a part.

Yet perhaps instrumental motivation or orientation should have a greater prominence in theory and research, at least in certain settings, most notably in *foreign language environments*. In the field of language learning, a foreign language is defined as one that is learned in a place where that language is not typically used as the medium of ordinary communication (for example, French as it is usually learned in the US). Foreign language learners are barraged by their own native language and have to go out of their way to find stimulation and input in the target language. These students typically receive input in the new language only in the classroom and by rather artificial means. Foreign language environments contrast with *second language settings*. In the area of language learning, a second language is defined as one that is learned in a location where that language is typically used as the main vehicle of everyday communication for most people (for instance, French being learned by a nonnative speaker of that language in France or in Francophone Africa or Canada). The learner of the second language is surrounded by stimulation, both visual and auditory, in the target language and thus has many motivational and instructional advantages. Much of the research on language learning motivation has taken place in Canada, in settings where people are learning the target language (French or English) as a second language.

The question of whether motivations differ between learners of second and foreign language is very important and has been repeatedly raised in recent years (Au, 1988; Crookes and Schmidt, 1991; Dörnyei, 1990a, 1990b; Horwitz, 1990; Oller, 1981b). For instance, Ely's empirical research findings (1986a, 1986b) within the US show three motivational clusters, the first two corresponding to integrative and instrumental and the third clearly centered on the need to fulfill a foreign language requirement (which might in fact also be considered an instrumental reason to learn the language).

Dörnyei (1990a, 1990b) suggests that instrumental motivation might be more important than integrative motivation for foreign language learners. According to Dörnyei, foreign language learners rarely have sufficient experience with the target language community to have clearly articulated attitudes toward that community, and they are therefore uncommitted to integrating with that group.

Along the lines of L2 researchers Au (1988), Crookes and Schmidt (1991), Horwitz (1990), and Oller (1981b), Dörnyei asserts that instrumental goals contribute significantly to motivation for foreign language learners (probably more than for second language learners). He also states that integrative reasons are, for foreign language learners, less specific to a particular target culture and are determined more by attitudes and beliefs about foreign language and cultures in general. This means that an inexperienced learner of German in the US might have a generalized interest in getting to know foreigners, but might not have a powerful urge to merge with the German society itself with which he or she has so far had no contact.

Dörnyei also states that instrumental motivation and need for achievement (which we discuss later) are associated with each other, and that these two factors affect foreign language students at an intermediate proficiency level and below. He suggests that integrative motivation might be necessary to go beyond the intermediate level in foreign language learning.

I agree that the motivations of foreign and second language learners are often highly disparate. I also agree that integrative motivation is much more meaningful for second language learners, who must learn to live in the new culture and communicate fluently in the target language, than for most foreign language learners, who are separated in space and attitude from the target culture and who rarely surpass intermediate language proficiency. Now I turn to the issue of definitions of motivation — the road signs we follow in our exploration.

CLEARER, MORE COMPREHENSIVE ROAD SIGNS NEEDED

Crookes and Schmidt (1991) suggest an expanded definition of L2 learning motivation. Using the work of Maehr and Archer (1987) and Keller (1983, pp. 289–320), Crookes and Schmidt suggest that motivation to learn a language has both internal and external features. This corresponds to the motivational system outlined by Cooley and Leinhardt (1975), containing internal and external motivators.

To Crookes and Schmidt, the structure of motivation includes four internal, attitudinal factors: (1) interest in the L2 based on existing attitudes, experience, and background knowledge on the learners' part; (2) relevance, which involves the perception that personal needs such as achievement, affiliation, and power are being met by learning the L2; (3) expectancy of success or failure; and (4) outcomes, i.e., the extrinsic or intrinsic rewards felt by the learner.

According to Crookes and Schmidt, external or behavioral characteristics include the fact that the learner: (1) decides to choose, pay attention to, and engage in L2 learning; (2) persists or perseveres in it over an extended period of time and returns to it after interruptions; and (3) maintains a high activity level. These factors are strikingly similar to empirical findings about motivation in the workplace, as will be shown later. Strikingly different is the famous model of school learning designed by Carroll in 1963. Perseverance (persistence) is the *only* motivational factor in Carroll's model, which includes aptitude, instructional clarity, perseverance, and learning opportunity as the four predictors of achievement. In contrast, the Crookes and Schmidt model shows perseverance as just one of seven important motivational factors that might influence achievement.

Dörnyei (1994a) emphasizes that many aspects of L2 learning motivation do not neatly fit into earlier paradigms. He stresses additional components, such as: (1) intrinsic and extrinsic motivation; (2) goal-setting; (3) cognitive components such as attribution theory, learned helplessness, and self-efficacy; (4) self-confidence; (5) need for achievement; and (6) course-specific, teacher-specific, and group-specific motivational components. Dörnyei also recommends ways to develop students' self-confidence and self-efficacy, decrease their anxiety, promote motivation-enhancing attributions, encourage students to set attainable subgoals, and increase the attractiveness of course content.

These ideas and recommendations from Crookes and Schmidt (1991) and Dörnyei (1994a) adumbrate my own theory expansion (see Chapter 6). These L2 researchers call for inclusion of need-achievement concepts, expectancy-value ideas, and attribution/self-efficacy constructs in an enlarged theory of L2 learning motivation.

SOCIAL PSYCHOLOGISTS BEGIN TO EXPAND THEIR MAIN HIGHWAY

Interestingly, Tremblay and Gardner (1995) have recently completed a study that includes many of these factors that I am calling for. This study expands upon all earlier versions of Gardner's Socio-Educational Model. The investigation tests and ultimately includes as important such "new" variables as goal salience (including goal specificity and goal-setting strategies), self-efficacy, and attributions about success or failure — along with the expected language attitudes, language dominance in the environment, motivational effort, desire to learn (or valence), and achievement.

This is a very significant expansion, which goes well beyond the previous bounds of the Socio-Educational Model and answers some of the main questions that have dogged the model in the past. This can be considered a major exploration of new pathways in language learning motivation. The model that is now being built by these researchers in no way destroys the social psychological base; instead, this base is used as a touchstone for new and important features that were not included before.

A CALL TO EXPLORE MORE AND WIDER PATHWAYS

This book calls for the exploration of more and wider pathways of language learning motivation. For instance, Chapter 2, by Richard Schmidt of the University of Hawai'i, Deena Boraie of the American University in Cairo, and Omneya Kassabgy of the Career Development Center in Cairo, provides an immensely rich review of research on language learning motivation, bringing insights from areas outside of the language field. These insights serve as background to a large empirical study conducted in Egypt that aims to elucidate the internal structures and internal connections of language learning motivation. The study uses factor analysis and multidimensional scaling to produce an exceptionally useful view of motivation in a foreign language setting. Egypt has many unique features that show up in the research results; however, it also has characteristics common to most other foreign language environments, and these characteristics reveal themselves in this chapter as well.

Chapter 3, by Zoltán Dörnyei of Eötvös University in Budapest, is a personalized view of language learning motivation research. Dörnyei explains his own involvement in this research in the last decade, starting with a social psychological approach and gradually adding new variables from other psychological fields. The reason these variables were added was that Dörnyei could not explain his foreign language results using just the variables in the social psychological model. He describes a recent study in which three distinct dimensions are identified: integrative motivation, linguistic self-confidence, and appraisal of the classroom environment. He then portrays three levels of motivation that arise from the study: the language level, the learner level, and the learning situation level. Specific and highly practical directions for future research are Dörnyei's final contribution.

In Chapter 4, Madeline Ehrman of the Foreign Service Institute describes a study of highly selected, well-educated adult language learners who are learning a variety of languages for government service. In this investigation, she reports on a survey-based investigation of many different aspects of motivation. The study shows that students and teachers perceive motivation in different ways. Teacher-perceived extrinsic motivation and student-perceived intrinsic motivation are linked to end-of-training proficiency outcomes. Motivation, according to the results, is more situation-specific or person-and-situation-specific than our written instrumentation and general constructs can show. Therefore, qualitative case information is also necessary to explain some seemingly contradictory or anomalous patterns.

Chapter 5, by Mayumi Okada of Hiroshima, Rebecca Oxford of the University of Alabama, and Suzuna Abo of Hobart and William Smith College, examines the motivation and learning strategies of native-English-speaking students of Japanese and Spanish. This chapter shows that students of the more difficult language, Japanese, are much more highly motivated and use a wider range of language learning strategies. Self-selection helps explain the reasons for this. Overall, the largest correlations between motivation and strategy use occur for metacognitive and cognitive strategies. Particular types of learning strategies are used by learners of each language due to factors such as the nature of the language, the degree and kind of motivation, and the classroom approach.

Rebecca Oxford and Jill Shearin present language learning motivation "in a new key." This involves a thorough consideration of motivational elements and issues drawn systematically from other areas of psychology (in addition to social psychology): general, educational, industrial, cognitive developmental, and sociocultural. The authors explain each component, such as goal-setting, and then show how it is applicable to language learning motivation. At the end of the chapter, the authors summarize detailed implications for language teachers and offer suggestions for future language learning motivation research. They thus call for a significant expansion of traditional concepts of language learning motivation.

GRATITUDE FOR THE GROUND WE TREAD
AND HOPE FOR FUTURE EXPLORATION

In this call for expansion, I am not asking for social psychological contributions to be thrown out or ignored. Indeed, not to push the metaphor too far, I might say that social psychologists such as Robert Gardner and his research colleagues have paved the way for us and provided us the sound footing that allows us to pursue other routes. As Dörnyei (1994b, p. 519) proclaims,

> I believe that the most important milestone in the history of L2 motivation research has been Gardner and Lambert's discovery that success is a function of the learner's attitude toward the linguistic-cultural community of the target language, thus adding a social dimension to the study of motivation to learn an L2... By combining motivation theory with social psychological theory, the model of L2 motivation that Gardner and Lambert developed was much more elaborate and advanced than many contemporary mainstream psychological models of motivation in that it was empirically testable and did indeed explain a considerable amount of variance in student motivation and achievement.

It is only because of such exceptional contributions that researchers now have the solid ground and the vantage point to see what else might be useful to add in the creation of an even more comprehensive theory of language learning motivation.

The current interchange of ideas does not have to be a battle of one side against the other. In fact, Gardner and Tremblay (1994b, p. 527) jocularly state: "It is our impression that just such a gathering of ideas is similar to the change that takes place just before a concert when isolated and dissonant notes suddenly change into a symphonic poem. Pass the wine, please!"

Perhaps this message signifies that investigators from different conceptual backgrounds can eventually learn to walk together on the same road. Multiple pathways can merge into a newly resurfaced, better lighted, easier-to-follow highway that shows us a clearer understanding of language learning motivation. On this road we can travel more readily and steadily with learners and teachers, who are the most important people of all in the language learning enterprise. The result of our joint exploration will be more effective and more satisfying language learning.

Richard Schmidt
The University of Hawai'i at Mānoa

Deena Boraie
The American University in Cairo

Omneya Kassabgy
Career Development Center, Cairo

CHAPTER 2

FOREIGN LANGUAGE MOTIVATION: INTERNAL STRUCTURE AND EXTERNAL CONNECTIONS

ABSTRACT

Thousands of adults enroll annually in private EFL courses in Egypt. What spurs these learners to exert the effort required and pay the fees in a country where access to public education is free at all levels? Our understanding of such issues is limited by the fact that most research on motivation has been conducted in second rather than foreign language learning contexts and in North American or European cultural settings. In the study reported here, a questionnaire was developed, based on current work on motivation in second and foreign language contexts and more general models from cognitive and educational psychology, and was administered to a sample of 1,554 adult learners at the Center for Adult and Continuing Education (CACE) at the American University in Cairo, with 1,464 questionnaires used for the analyses. Factor analysis and multidimensional scaling were used to identify the components of EFL motivation for this population. Results suggest that there are three basic dimensions to motivation for learning foreign languages, which we label Affect, Goal Orientation, and Expectancy. In general terms, these are probably universal and neurobiologically based, although the analysis suggests a specific Egyptian orientation with respect to the precise definition and content of each dimension. Learner profiles with respect to these dimensions of motivation were related to age, gender, and proficiency. Motivation is also related to learning strategies and preferences for certain kinds of classes and learning tasks. Those who scored high on the affective dimension of motivation preferred communicatively oriented language classes, while those high in anxiety tended not to like group work or other aspects of currently popular communicative language pedagogy. Students with a traditional approach to learning (e.g., choosing memorization strategies over inferencing from context) also preferred classes in which the teacher maintains control.

Schmidt, Richard, Boraie, Deena, & Kassabgy, Omneya (1996). Foreign language motivation: Internal structure and external connections. In Rebecca Oxford (Ed.), *Language Learning Motivation: Pathways to the New Century*. (Technical Report #11) (pp. 9–70). Honolulu: University of Hawai'i, Second Language Teaching & Curriculum Center.

INTRODUCTION

The research reported here was stimulated by both practical and theoretical considerations in the field of foreign language learning and teaching. The topic of motivation is of practical interest to language program designers and administrators, who want to attract students to programs that will motivate them to learn by being congruent with their needs and interests, to teachers, who would like to use pedagogical techniques that reinforce and develop student motivation, and to learners themselves, who must sometimes struggle to maintain their internal motivation in order to persist in the inherently difficult task of learning a foreign language. Our initial interest in investigating EFL motivation was prompted by the following question: What spurs thousands of Egyptians to exert the effort required and pay the fees for private instruction in English? The specific context within which we asked this question was the program of EFL classes in the Center for Adult and Continuing Education (CACE) at the American University in Cairo, which enrolls over 10,000 adults annually and which is only one of many programs offering classes in English in Egypt. Although we do not claim that our results generalize beyond the context of adult Egyptian learners, personally financed language classes are common in many European and Asian nations, and future research may identify commonalities with the Egyptian case.

English is stressed in Egyptian education at all levels. It is taught as a foreign language in government schools starting at grade six and as a second language starting in kindergarten in private "language schools," which are attended by large numbers of learners. English is the medium of instruction in most tertiary education, including colleges of medicine, engineering, science, and agriculture. However, in spite of the fact that English is an integral component of the Egyptian school curriculum and that, across the board, access to public education in Egypt is free, thousands of adults enroll annually in EFL evening classes. This indicates a high level of motivation among Egyptian adults attached to achieving proficiency in English.

Earlier research (Kassabgy, 1976) established that Egyptian adult EFL learners demonstrated positive attitudes toward English, along with instrumental motivation to learn the foreign language with the major objective of emigrating to the West. These results were a direct reflection of the socio-economic conditions of Egypt at that time. Today, two decades later, in spite of the fact that the emigration motive is far less pertinent, increasing numbers of adults still enroll in EFL programs. We look to motivational factors that will explain this phenomenon, but the motives of Egyptian adult EFL learners have become more complex. EFL motivation cannot be viewed simply as the instrumental drive to emigrate in order to lead a better life abroad, and the ability to communicate fluently in English brings with it promises of a better life within Egypt. English ability is associated with educational achievement, which in turn determines social status. Prestigious professions require a certain level of proficiency in English, and career advancement in Egypt in many fields is affected by the ability to communicate fluently in English.

Discussions among teachers and administrators had identified several possible types of motivation among this learner population. It was felt that for some learners, especially housewives, learning English provides a chance to get out of the house and meet other people. Secondary and university students, it was felt, are primarily motivated by instrumental reasons, to get a job or to work for a joint venture company. Some learners seem to have a fantasy motive, a conviction that life will be better (in unspecified ways) if they learn English. Social pressures (from parents, peers, or supervisors) are probably factors for some learners. However, no recent studies exist that deal with this population. A second reason for investigating motivation in this context was that in this program and in many others, a high drop-out rate had been observed, and no reasons had been found to explain why close to 50% of all students fail to complete the courses in which they enroll. Could this be understood, we wondered, from an examination of motivational factors? Do learners with some motivational profiles succeed better than others at language learning and persist longer in the endeavor (Dörnyei, 1990a; Gardner and Smythe, 1975; Ramage, 1990)? Might some initially motivated learners encounter a lack of fit between their self-perceived interests, needs, goals, and expectations and what they encounter in classes? If so, this would have implications for classroom methodology and teacher training.

The present research does not attempt to answer all of the above questions. Because our research design is cross-sectional rather than longitudinal, we have not attempted to investigate the dynamic interplay between motivational factors and what goes on in the foreign language classroom day by day, and because the analyses reported here are based on quantitative rather than qualitative data, we focus on trends across learners rather than the complex interaction of social, cultural, and psychological factors within individual learners. But even to begin investigating these practically oriented questions runs up immediately against some crucial theoretical issues. What do we mean by motivation? How do we recognize it and measure it? Is it a unitary concept, or does it have several or many facets? Can motivation for language learning be thought of in the same way in second language learning environments and in foreign language learning contexts where students have little or no exposure to the target language outside of class? Is motivation universal or cross-culturally variable? Can models developed in the US and Canada be applied in Egypt, where Western cultural values are generally felt to be alien?

MODELS OF MOTIVATION

Keller (1983) identified ability and motivation as the major sources of variation in educational success. Ability refers to what a person can do; motivation, to what a person will do. Johnson (1979) referred to motivation as the "tendency to expend effort to achieve goals" (p. 283). One implication of these views is that, whatever its sources might be, motivation is motivation, something that exists (in varying strength) or does not exist (Bardwell and Braaksma, 1983) and which can be measured by observing behavior. Maehr and Archer (1987) identified some of the key behavioral aspects of motivation: direction (decisions to attend to some things and not to others), persistence (concentrating attention or action on an activity for an extended duration), continued motivation (returning to an activity without being obliged to), and activity level (intensity of effort).

Many researchers treat motivation as a single construct. Research done under the influence of goal-setting theory emphasizes that a single factor, acceptance of difficult but achievable goals, has a powerful influence on behavior (Locke and Latham, 1984). Need-achievement theorists have usually assessed motivation in educational settings from the perspective of a single construct (Atkinson, 1974, Nicholls, 1984), as have attribution theorists (Weiner, 1985). Others combine multiple measures of motivation together in order to arrive at a single score or theoretical concept. In the field of foreign and second language learning, this approach is evident in the work of Krashen (1981, 1985), who collapses several kinds of motivation into the more general construct of an affective filter, and in Schumann's acculturation model (Schumann, 1986, pp. 379–392), where different types of motivation are combined with such varied social and psychological factors as group size and culture shock to arrive at a superordinate construct called acculturation, which according to the model predicts the degree to which learners will or will not acquire a second language.

Other theorists and researchers have found that it is important to look at motivation not as a single construct or as a list of different types of motivation combined in "soup-pot" fashion, but as a multifactor trait. Bardwell and Braaksma (1983) observe that investigating the style of that trait or interrelationships among the various factors will allow researchers and practitioners to observe finer differences in the ways people approach problems and is especially important in education, since different learner needs and motivation styles are probably at least as relevant for pedagogy as students' differing learning styles. At the same time, since there is a potentially unlimited number of reasons one might study a foreign language and factors that might influence motivation, some reductionism is inevitable. Among the major theories that consider more than a single motivational construct, some are dichotomous (two-factor) models, while others view motivation from a multifactorial perspective. For reasons of space, we will review briefly only a few examples of each type.

The best known constructs concerning motivation for second language learning are those of integrative and instrumental motivation, based primarily on the important work of Gardner (1985b, 1989). An instrumental orientation results from recognition of the practical advantages of learning and is identified when learners say that they want to learn the target language to pass examinations or for economic or social advancement. An integrative orientation is identified when learners state that they want to learn a foreign language because they are attracted to the target language culture or group or the language itself. The integrative orientation implies an interest in interacting with target language speakers, and may but does not necessarily include willingness or desire to actually integrate into the target language group. The integrative motive (not quite the same as the integrative orientation; see Chapter 6 in this volume and Gardner and MacIntyre, 1991, for discussion) is identified when learners also indicate a readiness to act toward those goals. Although these two motivational factors are sometimes seen as being in opposition to each other (i.e., classifying learners as integratively or instrumentally motivated), this is not necessarily the case, since one can find learners who are both instrumentally and integratively motivated to learn a foreign language and those with neither type of motivation, as well as learners who score high on one type of motivation and low on the other.

Gardner's model of the ways in which motivation for foreign language learning operates in educational settings has been summarized (Au, 1988; Gardner, 1988) in terms of five hypotheses:

- The integrative motive hypothesis: Integrative motivation is positively associated with second language achievement.

- The cultural belief hypothesis: Cultural beliefs influence the development of the integrative motive and the degree to which integrativeness and achievement are related.

- The active learner hypothesis: Integratively motivated learners are successful because they are active learners.

- The causality hypothesis: Integrative motivation is a cause; second language achievement, the effect.

- The two process hypothesis: Aptitude and integrative motivation are independent factors in second language learning.

Research based on this model has been very useful, but a number of criticisms have been raised against the particular view of motivation incorporated in it, as well as some of the hypotheses advanced by Gardner. While Gardner has consistently emphasized the support that integrative motivation offers for language learning, this does not seem to be the case in all language learning settings. When integrative motive has been measurable, virtually every possible relationship has been found between this type of motive and language proficiency: positive, negative, nil, and ambiguous (Au, 1988). With respect to the active learner hypothesis, if integratively motivated learners are successful because they are active learners, then the same might be theorized of successful instrumentally oriented learners. It is also unclear from many studies whether motivation is the cause or the result of successful learning. These and other criticisms of this model have been summarized by Au (1988), Crookes and Schmidt (1991), Oller (1981) and Oller and Perkins (1980).

Although developed within the Canadian second language context, this model has been extended to other second language contexts (Kraemer, 1993) and has been very influential in the foreign language literature as well. However, it cannot be assumed that the same model is appropriate to foreign language contexts such as Egypt, where learners are limited to interacting in the target language within the confines of the classroom. In addition, many Egyptian learners find the cultural values of the target language community (the United States and/or Britain) to be alien. The model also leaves out many possible influences on motivation (Crookes and Schmidt; 1991; Dörnyei, 1990a; Oxford and Shearin, 1994; Skehan, 1989). After considering learners he has known over the years in Egypt and the Ivory Coast and reflecting on his own study of Egyptian hieroglyphs (a dead language that offers no opportunities for integration and few if any instrumental advantages), Bagnole (1993) noted that there must be more to motivation than instrumental and integrative goals.

Another dichotomous model of motivation may shed light on Bagnole's experiences with hieroglyphs. The contrast between intrinsic and extrinsic motivation is well known in psychology (deCharms, 1968; Deci, Vallerand, Pelletier, and Ryan, 1991; Deci and Ryan, 1985; Lepper and Greene, 1978). Extrinsic motivation is motivation to do something because of an external reward that may be obtained, while intrinsic motivation is demonstrated when we do something because we get rewards enough from the activity itself. The extrinsic-intrinsic distinction is somewhat similar to the instrumental-integrative distinction, but it is not identical, and both instrumental and integrative motivation are properly seen as subtypes of extrinsic motivation, since both are concerned with goals or outcomes. We can easily imagine a situation in which a learner wants to master a language in order to interact with native speakers of that language but nevertheless does not actually enjoy studying the language, an activity for which he or she has only an extrinsic, goal-oriented motivation ([+integrative] [–intrinsic]). We can equally imagine learners with instrumental motivation, for example, to satisfy a language requirement, who do enjoy studying and learning the language ([–integrative] [+instrinsic]), as well as learners with no clear reasons for studying a language who find language learning interesting and pleasurable nevertheless ([–instrumental] [–integrative] [+intrinsic]). It is also possible for a learner to be intrinsically motivated in an activity for its own sake ([+intrinsic]) while simultaneously appreciating its practical rewards ([+extrinsic]). The worst possible situation is one in which a learner has neither type of motivation for foreign language learning, neither enjoying the activity for its own sake nor thinking that it will bring any useful results ([–integrative] [–instrumental] [–intrinsic] [–extrinsic]).

Positing a construct of intrinsic motivation leads to more questions. What makes an activity intrinsically motivating? Why are some activities intensely enjoyable, while others make us bored or anxious? One answer to these questions has been given by the psychologist Mihaly Csikszentmihalyi (Csikszentmihalyi and Nakamura, 1989; Wong and Csikszentmihalyi, 1991). Csikszentmihalyi has examined the ebb and flow of psychological states (motivation, concentration, involvement) in daily experience and has proposed a theory in which the challenge of an activity (as perceived by the person doing it) and the level of skill brought by the person to the activity (also subjectively evaluated) are the crucial determinants of psychological states.

Csikszentmihalyi's theory predicts that motivation, affect, arousal, and concentration will all be highest when challenge and skill are perceived to be about equal and when both are high. When the challenge of a task is high and skills are low, the resulting psychological state is anxiety. When challenge is low and skills are high, the outcome is boredom, and when both challenge and skill are low, the outcome is the negative state of apathy. The model has received support from case studies as well as a number of studies with large sample sizes involving people of various cultures, ages, and social classes, in both the United States and Europe. The relationships among the variables of challenge, skill, and motivation (as well as affective, arousal, and concentration variables) have been claimed to be universal (Csikszentmihalyi and Nakamura, 1989). This model of motivation is an attractive one, because it suggests a psychological analog to Krashen's "i+1" principle for the learning of grammar (Krashen, 1985). Krashen has argued that second language acquisition depends upon input to the learner containing grammatical structures that are just beyond the learner's current competence. Csikszentmihalyi's theory predicts that challenging activities that are just beyond a learner's current level of skill will be intrinsically motivating.

Others have proposed multifactor models of motivation, usually derived by factor analysis from responses to a wide-ranging motivational questionnaire. One such model is that of Dörnyei (1990a), based on research carried out in Hungary, described by Dörnyei as a typical European foreign language learning environment. Dörnyei posited a motivational construct consisting of (1) an instrumental motivational subsystem; (2) an integrative motivational subsystem, a multifaceted cluster with four dimensions (general interest in foreign languages, a desire to broaden one's view and avoid provincialism, a desire for new stimuli and challenges, and a travel orientation); (3) need for achievement; and (4) attributions about past failures. Schumann (1994a, 1994b) has suggested that Dörnyei's multifactor model is complementary to a model in which stimulus situations are evaluated in the brain according to five criteria: novelty, pleasantness, goal or need significance, coping mechanisms, and self and social image. In Schumann's view, constructs at the psychological level such as integrative and instrumental motivation and Dörnyei's more detailed model are, at the neurobiological level, the products of the brain's appraisal system aggregated across individuals. Because each individual's experience is different, each individual's stimulus appraisal system will be different and cannot be identified or responded to pedagogically.

Another study that used a broad conception of motivation, based on the work of Boekaerts (1987, 1989), was a research project carried out among Finnish sixth and eighth grade children studying English conducted by Julkunen (1989). Julkunen investigated both trait (relatively stable) and state (fluctuating) motivation in connection with student competence and attributional processes. Factor analysis of an extensive background questionnaire indicated that students' general foreign language motivation could be described in terms of eight factors: (1) a communicative motive, including aspects of integrative, instrumental, and cognitive motivation but emphasizing the function of language as a means of communication; (2) classroom level intrinsic motivation, including liking for challenging tasks; (3) teacher/method motivation, including liking and disliking of certain teaching methods; (4) integrative motivation, reflected in positive attitudes toward English and American culture; (5) a helplessness factor; (6) an anxiety factor; (7) criteria for success/failure, i.e., an attributional factor; and (8) latent interest in learning English.

Finally, in an expansion of Gardner's earlier socio-educational model, Tremblay and Gardner (1995) have proposed the incorporation of measures of effort, attention, persistence, self-efficacy, confidence, valence, causal attributions, and goal-setting in studies of motivation for language learning and have applied the model successfully to an investigation of learning a first language (French) in a bilingual community (Ontario).

CULTURAL INFLUENCES ON MOTIVATION

There is little doubt that cultural influences have some affect on motivation and reason to suspect that this influence may be large (Markus and Kitayama, 1991). We know from research in social psychology that the answers that informants give on questionnaires will be affected not only by their "true" attitudes, attributions, and expressions of interests, but also by their conceptions of an ideal self, which are partly individualistic but also heavily influenced by cultural values (Todd, 1995). A more serious problem arises if particular theories of motivation turn out to be ethnocentric. This charge has been leveled most frequently at theories of achievement motivation (Castanell, 1984; Maehr and Nicholls, 1980) and attribution theory (Duda and Allison, 1989; Kashima and Triandis, 1986; Murphy-Berman and Sharma, 1987). Komin (1990) comments that since people's values and belief systems are culturally conditioned, authors of theories of motivation are no exception. "Thus, American theories reflect American culture, and Italian theories reflect Italian culture, etc." (p. 702). Weiner (1991) emphasized that theories of motivation typically reflect culturally based metaphors, for example, person as machine (in Freudian and drive theory), person as a rational decision maker (in some value/expectancy theories), or person as scientist (in attribution theories).

Csikszentmihalyi's prediction that challenge and skill are the primary determinants of motivation and other psychological states was investigated with respect to Thai learners of English by Schmidt and Savage (1992), whose results did not support the theory. In that study, there was evidence that some learners were intrinsically motivated, but there were no significant correlations, either positive or negative, between learners' ratings of the level of challenge in a particular activity or their skill in doing it and on-line measures of motivation, affect, or psychological activation. Schmidt and Savage concluded that the balance between the challenge of an activity and one's ability level may be one factor contributing to motivation, but it is not of overwhelming importance for Thai learners. Instead of arising from a single variable that outweighs all others, whether or not an activity is considered enjoyable and intrinsically motivating by Thais seems to depend on a large number of factors, including an ego orientation, the importance of smooth interpersonal relationships and harmony, a competence orientation characterized by a perception of education as a means to climb the social ladder, an interdependence orientation, and a fun-pleasure orientation (Komin, 1990). Based on these findings, it seems that Csikszentmihalyi's reductionist model of intrinsic motivation is too simplistic, because intrinsic motivation and its associated psychological states arise from many interacting factors rather than one or two, and ethnocentric, because of the assumption that the psychological sources of intrinsic motivation are universal rather than culture-specific.

MOTIVATION AND COGNITIVE PROCESSES

Other than Gardner's hypothesis that integratively motivated learners succeed because they are active learners (Gardner, 1985b, 1988) and Schumann's theoretical connections between motivation, interaction, and the provision of comprehensible input (Schumann, 1986), it is rather remarkable that theories of foreign language learning have been generally silent about how motivation works, in terms of the mechanisms of acquisition. It is equally remarkable that there has been so little research exploring the links between motivation and cognitive processes.

Much more remains to be done in this area, drawing on work on motivation and cognitive processing in educational contexts other than language learning. A theoretical model relating motivational factors, cognitive factors, and learning outcomes for academic subjects has been developed by Pintrich (1988, 1989) and could be explored in connection with foreign language learning. Pintrich has specified those aspects of cognition that are important for educational success:

- Cognitive strategies involve the psychological mechanism of attention focusing, the necessary and sufficient condition for encoding into memory (Carr and Curran, 1994; Logan, 1988); Schmidt, 1993, 1995; Tomlin and Villa, 1994). Basic cognitive strategies include rehearsal (such as saying material aloud when reading, copying material into a notebook, or underlining), elaboration (paraphrasing, summarizing, note-taking), and organizational strategies (e.g., selecting the main idea from a text).

- Metacognitive strategies concern the control and regulation of cognition. Basic strategies include planning (for example, setting goals for studying), monitoring (for example, self-testing to ensure comprehension), and self-regulation (for example, re-reading or reviewing material).

- Resource management strategies include time management, space management, and strategies that call on the support of others. For example, good learners know when they don't know something, and will ask teachers for help or consult textbooks or dictionaries.

Pintrich (1989) has carried out research identifying relationships among motivational factors, cognitive strategies, and educational success in American university courses. Schiefele (1991) explored the relationships between one motivational factor, interest, and the use of learning strategies in first language reading, finding that interest correlated positively with the use of elaboration and information-seeking strategies and negatively with rehearsal, but did not affect organization or time management strategies. But none of this research has yet concerned foreign language learning. Within the foreign language field, there has been research concerning the links between cognitive strategies, usually called learning strategies, and learning outcomes (O'Malley and Chamot, 1990), but little research so far linking aspects of motivation with the use of such learning strategies. (For exceptions, see Oxford and Nyikos, 1989, in which motivation was the strongest influence on strategy use; Ehrman and Oxford, 1995, in which strategy use was correlated significantly and sometimes strongly with motivational factors; and Chapter 5 in this volume.)

MOTIVATION AND INSTRUCTIONAL DESIGN

Keller (1983) has referred to motivation as the "neglected heart of instructional design" (p. 390). Crookes and Schmidt (1991) identified some of the ways in which motivational factors can be related to classroom techniques, as well as to curriculum and syllabus design. Interest can be enhanced by using varied materials, by starting lessons with questions that put the learner into a problem-solving mode, by relating instructional material to topics already of interest to learners, and by the use of paradoxes and puzzles. In general, interest is fostered by personalizing material and by focusing on the concrete rather than the abstract. Relevance can be enhanced by analyzing and addressing learner needs and goals in language study, as well as by addressing such basic human needs as the need for achievement, for affiliation, and for power. Self-confidence and expectations of success can be enhanced by increasing students' experience with success, by making clear the requirements of a language course, by setting learning goals that are challenging but realistic, and by maximizing student control over outcomes, so that students see success as the product of their own efforts. Feedback can be an important factor (either positive or negative) that affects student motivation. Corrective feedback (error correction) that simply tells a student that he or she has made an error can be very discouraging, which is one reason many teachers are reluctant to correct student errors at all. It can be argued that the best feedback is that which is provided when it is most useful for the student, usually just before the same task is presented again. A well timed reminder of points to be watchful of and errors to be avoided can help students to carry out a particular learning task more successfully. In other words, feedback that promotes success is motivating; feedback that merely signals failure is demotivating. Additional strategies for enhancing motivation in foreign language classes have been proposed by Dörnyei (1994a) Oxford and Shearin (1994) and Fotos (1994), but as Gardner and Tremblay (1994a) have pointed out, none of these suggestions has been accompanied by empirical findings showing that they are effective.

There has been almost no research investigating relationships between the motivational styles of language learners and the types of classrooms and learning tasks that are consonant with those styles. Ames (1984, 1992) observed that although cooperative learning structures have been widely touted in the educational literature as good for promoting achievement and self-esteem for all learners, the situation is somewhat more complex. Competitive, cooperative, and individualistic goal structures elicit different types of motivation, and students who have been socialized into different motivational styles may prefer different learning structures.

There probably are other links between motivation and pedagogical aspects of language teaching that are also worth exploring. Burnaby and Sun (1989) discussed the views of Chinese teachers toward communicative language teaching in the context of the wider curriculum, traditional teaching methods, class sizes, and schedules, as well as the communicative needs of learners, arguing that there is considerable support for the teachers' view that communicative methods are not relevant for most students' needs. They do not discuss the views of learners (as opposed to teachers) toward appropriate methodologies or make an explicit link to motivation, but it is likely that learners with different perceived needs and goals will be differentially receptive to certain methods and activities. Brindley (1989) pointed out that learners often have rather fixed ideas about what it means to be a learner and to learn a language, and Nunan (1989b) found that teachers and learners in migrant education programs in Australia had quite different attitudes toward specific classroom activities and tasks. While teachers accepted the value of communicatively oriented activities, the learners surveyed placed greater value on traditional learning activities. Teachers gave higher ratings to such activities as using pictures, films, and videos, student self-discovery of errors, and pair work, while students gave higher ratings to vocabulary development, pronunciation practice, and external error correction. Whether learner expectations are met with respect to classroom methods and activities may have a wash-back effect on motivation as well. Learners who are motivated to learn English only to pass a state exam might well prefer a traditional, teacher-centered, grammar-focused class and may feel they are not learning in communicatively oriented classes. Learners who are integratively motivated may be more receptive to communicative approaches and may suffer a severe drop in interest in language courses if the focus is primarily on grammar (Schmidt and Frota, 1986).

There has been some investigation of learner attitudes toward such instructional factors in second and foreign language contexts (Kern, 1995), independent of any connection to motivation, but the only study we are aware of that explicitly links motivation and instructional tasks is Julkunen's (1989) study of Finnish learners of English. In that study, students performed three closed tasks (tasks for which there was only one correct answer) and three open tasks (tasks for which various answers were possible) related to English vocabulary in three different learning situations created by instructions and seating arrangements: individualistic, cooperative, and competitive. Students' pre-task and post-task appraisals of these tasks were recorded through an on-line motivation questionnaire. Results showed that students were more liable to perceive themselves as failures in open tasks than in closed tasks, perhaps because it was more difficult for students to assess results in terms of success and failure in open tasks. High achievers evaluated all three learning situations (individualistic, competitive, and cooperative) positively, particularly in the closed tasks. The cooperative learning situation emerged as the best learning situation for all students in terms of its effects on motivation.

RESEARCH GOALS

This study attempts to achieve the following goals:

- To identify the components of foreign language learning motivation for a population of adult EFL learners in Egypt;

- To identify the components of learner preferences for specific classroom practices and activities for the same population of EFL learners;

- To identify the components of learning strategies that are reportedly used by the same population;

- To identify relationships between the components of motivation and preferred classroom learning activities; and

- To identify relationships between the components of motivation and learning strategies.

Because of the wide variety of factors that might be expected to influence motivation for foreign language learning, this study explores the concept of foreign language motivation within a broad conception of motivation that avoids premature reductionism or assumes that all aspects of motivation are universal. The model of motivation used was a composite of several current models, especially those of Pintrich (1989), deCharms (1968), Keller (1983), Maehr and Archer (1987), and Dörnyei (1990a). These models fall generally within the broad category of value-expectancy theories of motivation. Such models assume that motivation is a multiplicative function of values and expectations. People will approach activities that they consider valuable and relevant to their personal goals and that they expect to succeed at.

The components of motivation investigated in this study included:

- Intrinsic goal orientation toward English

- Extrinsic goal orientation toward English

- Personal psychological goals of achievement and affiliation

- Expectation of success

- Attribution of success and failure

- Attitudes toward Americans and British speakers of English

- Attitudes toward American and British culture

- Anxiety

INFORMANTS

The informants for this study were 1,554 adult learners of EFL at the American University in Cairo, Center for Adult and Continuing Education, downtown and Heliopolis campuses, who completed a 100-item questionnaire. Questionnaires from subjects who failed to complete at least 80% of the items were discarded, resulting in a total of 1,502 questionnaires used for initial analysis. Another 38 questionnaires were discarded due to unavailability of background information, resulting in a total of 1,464 questionnaires used in the final analysis.

Table 1 displays the descriptive statistics on background variables for the 1,464 informants whose questionnaires were used for analysis. As can be seen in Table 1, 54% of the sample were males and 46% were females. Informants ranged in age from 15 to 70, but 58% were young adults (23–35), and another 24% were of university age. Informants were fairly evenly distributed across six different proficiency levels, from basic to advanced. More than half had completed university education, and a wide range of occupations was represented. The single largest occupational category was "unemployed" (20%). This partly reflects economic conditions in the country, but may be misleading because the number includes an unknown number of recently graduated students waiting to hear about positions.

Table 1: Descriptive statistics for 1,464 informants

Sex:		
Males		792
Females		672
Total		**1,464**
Age:		
15–18 (secondary school age)		69
19–22 (university age)		347
23–35 (young adults)		840
35+ (mature adults)		192
Total	(16 missing cases)	**1,448**
Proficiency level:		
Basic		208
Elementary		359
Lower intermediate		302

continued...

Table 1: Descriptive statistics for 1,464 informants (cont.)

Intermediate		230
Upper intermediate		205
Advanced		160
Total		**1,464**
Highest level of education completed:		
Pre-secondary		49
Secondary		188
Vocational training		405
BA./B.Sc.		766
MA./Ph.D.		26
Post graduate diploma		29
Total	(1 missing case)	**1,463**
Occupation:		
Unemployed		292
Accountant/auditor		233
Students		185
Secretary/clerk/receptionist		170
Professionals, lawyers		167
Teachers, professors, researchers		105
Technical workers, systems analysts		101
Managers, senior administrators		56
Sales & marketing		55
Service industry workers		39
Police, security officers		26
Housewives		16
Journalism/mass media		9
Musician/artist		7
Total	(3 missing cases)	**1,461**

Number of English courses previously taken		
None		428
1–2		527
3–10		473
11–19		35
Total	(1 missing case)	**1,463**

Since the available subject access time was limited to a single class session, it was necessary to choose between probing a few concepts thoroughly and sampling a wider variety of concepts more tentatively. The latter was considered more appropriate for exploratory analysis. A 100-item questionnaire was constructed, on which students indicated their agreement or disagreement with various statements on six-point Likert scales. Six-point scales were used to eliminate neutral responses.

The questionnaire was administered in Arabic. A preliminary version of the questionnaire items was initially formulated in English, based on existing questionnaires in use, concepts of motivation found in the psychological literature, and discussions with teachers, administrators, and students. These questions were then professionally translated into Arabic, first literally and then more figuratively, in order to ensure that all questions were phrased in a way that was natural and appropriate. The Arabic version of the questionnaire was then back-translated to English. The Arabic version of the questionnaire is found in Appendix A. For the English back-translation, see Appendix B.

The first 50 items of the questionnaire concern motivation; the next set of 22 items concerns preferences for classroom instructional activities; and the final 25 items concern learning strategies. Three additional items were deleted from the analysis (see "analysis").

In Part A: Motivation, the first five items deal with intrinsic motivation, three of which are positively worded (e.g., *I enjoy learning English very much*), two of which are negatively worded (e.g., *I don't enjoy learning English, but I know that learning English is important for me*) and were reverse-coded for the analysis. Items #6 through 20 deal with extrinsic motivation and represent a variety of reasons for learning English (e.g., *Being able to speak English will add to my social status; I want to learn English because it is useful when traveling in many countries; I need to be able to read textbooks in English*). Items #21–24 concern personal psychological needs, both achievement-oriented (e.g., *I really want to learn more English in this class than I have done in the past*) and affiliation-oriented (e.g., *One of the most important things in this class is getting along with other students*). Items #26–34 concern expectations (e.g., *This English class will definitely help me improve my English*) and a number of locus of control statements (e.g., *If I do well in this course, it will be because I try hard; If I don't do well in this class, it will be because the class is too difficult)*. These items raise some interesting questions regarding their expression in Arabic, since Arabic culture and American-European culture (within which attribution theories have been formulated) stress very different views about personal volition. In most contexts in Arabic, positive statements about the future are obligatorily followed by the expression *insha'allah* ("God willing"), and whether to include this and other similar phrases in surveys has been of concern to social scientists. Tessler, Palmer, Farah, and Ibrahim (1987) reported that responses differ systematically depending on whether God is mentioned, so it is important to be consistent within a questionnaire. We chose to omit such explicit references, but noted that some informants qualified their positive responses to items asserting personal control over success and failure with marginal notes referring to God's will.

Questionnaire items #35–38 concern stereotypical attitudes toward Americans and British, which were elicited directly from a sample of students. Items #39–44 concern anxiety, including general class anxiety, speaking anxiety, test anxiety, and fear of the opinions of the teacher and other students. Items #45–50 concern motivational strength (e.g., *My attendance in this class will be good; I can honestly say that I really put my best effort into trying to learn English*).

Part B of the questionnaire contains 22 items dealing with preferences for instructional activities and other characteristics of the EFL class, including the use of Arabic and English in class, skill emphasis, a concern for communicative proficiency versus preparation for exams, teacher-fronted versus student-centered orientations, preferences for individualistic or cooperative and active or passive learning situations, attitudes toward challenging tasks, and preferences concerning feedback.

Part C of the questionnaire concerns cognitive strategies. Based primarily on the work of Pintrich (1989), the 25 items cover rehearsal and rote learning strategies (#1–4); elaboration (#5–7); organizational strategies (#8–9); inferencing strategies (#10–13); metacognitive strategies such as planning, monitoring, and regulating (#14–19); and resource management (#20–25).

PROCEDURES

To counterbalance any tiredness effects, three orderings of the questionnaire items were compiled and were randomly assigned to subjects for completion. Students completed the questionnaires in a single class period during the first week of the term.

ANALYSIS

After administration of the questionnaire and before analyzing the data, the questionnaire was validated by running a Pearson correlation matrix of the components of the motivation subscales and the items themselves. As a result the following three negatively worded items were deleted:

The English tend to be snobbish and unfriendly people.
Americans are not conservative.
American culture is not a very good influence in Egypt.

The internal consistency reliability of the components of motivation, attitudes toward instructional activities, and learning strategies were assessed by means of Cronbach's alpha coefficient. These are indicated on the English back-translation of the questionnaire in Appendix B. The data relating to EFL motivation, preferences for classroom activities, and learning strategies were then subjected to two different data reduction techniques. In the first of these, the data were factor analyzed (principal component analysis, SYSTAT 4.0) to extract underlying factors. The second analysis consisted of multidimensional scaling (MDS) of the same data. ANOVAs were used to assess the effects of age, gender, and proficiency on the dimensions of motivation that emerged from the MDS analysis, and Pearson product-moment correlations were used to examine relationships among motivational factors, instructional preferences, and preferred learning strategies.

RESULTS

Means and standard deviations for each of the questionnaire items are indicated on the back-translated English version of the questionnaire in Appendix B. Table 2 lists the most agreed with and least agreed with statements from Part A (motivation) of the questionnaire. From Table 2, it can be seen that the informants in this sample of Egyptian adult EFL learners expressed strong agreement with statements that they expect to do well in the course, that learning English is important, useful, and enjoyable, and that they expect to attend regularly and will probably take another course. These informants, in general, responded that they were not taking the class to please others (spouse, supervisor, other), to emigrate, or to pass examinations. They disagreed quite strongly with statements concerning anxiety. Although some items have high standard deviations, most informants in this sample said that they are not afraid of the opinions of teachers or fellow students and do not feel embarrassed or uncomfortable when speaking English.

These data are interesting, and we suspect that EFL teachers with considerable international experience (or experience in working with different cultural groups in second language settings) may see in this something of the motivational style of Egyptian learners, who are generally confident and committed to learning English. This might be contrasted with the different styles of other cultural groups, for example, Japanese learners of English, who are often excellent language learners but who frequently express a lack of confidence in their abilities, either because they truly do lack confidence or because it is socially appropriate to say that they do. However, since this is not a comparative study and because we are concerned more with the internal structure of motivation, these areas of agreement among our informants are of less central interest than areas of variation within their responses. These were analyzed through factor analysis and multidimensional scaling.

Table 2: Most and least agreed with statements from the motivation questionnaire

Item	Mean	SD
Highest agreement		
This English class will definitely help me improve my English.	5.604	0.706
I really want to learn more English in this class than I have in the past.	5.588	0.741
I enjoy learning English very much.	5.580	0.763
English is important to me because it will broaden my view.	5.568	0.813
I plan to continue studying English for as long as possible.	5.444	0.868
I'm learning English to become more educated.	5.428	0.947
My relationship with the teacher in this class is important to me.	5.378	0.906
I want to learn English because it is useful when traveling in many countries.	5.336	1.026
My attendance in this class will be good.	5.317	0.835
After this class I will probably take another course.	5.301	1.037
Least agreement		
If I don't do well in this class, it will be because the class is too difficult.	2.846	1.309
The main reason I am taking this class is that my parents/my spouse/my supervisors want me to improve my English.	2.693	1.826
I feel uncomfortable if I have to speak in my English class.	2.634	1.541
I want to learn English because I would like to emigrate.	2.552	1.738
It embarrasses me to volunteer answers in my English class.	2.541	1.480
I don't like to speak often in English class because I am afraid that my teacher will think I am not a good student.	2.455	1.493

I am afraid other students will laugh at me when I speak English.	2.223	1.403
The main reason I need to learn English is to pass examinations.	2.044	1.334

RESULTS OF THE FACTOR ANALYSES

The data from Parts A (motivation), B (preferences for instructional activities), and C (learning strategies) of the questionnaire were factor analyzed separately, using principal component analysis (SYSTAT 4.0) to extract underlying factors. The number of factors to be extracted was based on the following criteria:

- Minimum eigenvalues of 1.0
- Each factor to account for at least 3% of total variance
- Each factor to contain individual items with a minimum loading of .45

MOTIVATIONAL FACTORS

After varimax rotation, a nine-factor solution was chosen, which accounted for 48.3% of the total variance in the motivation subtest (see Table 3).

Table 3: Factor analysis for Part A: Motivation

	Label	Eigenvalue	Variance	Cumulative variance
Factor 1	Determination	10.44	12.9	12.9
Factor 2	Anxiety	3.52	6.2	19.1
Factor 3	Instrumental motivation	2.08	6.0	25.2
Factor 4	Sociability	1.21	5.3	30.5
Factor 5	Attitudes to culture	1.63	4.1	34.6
Factor 6	Foreign residence	1.17	3.7	38.3
Factor 7	Intrinsic motivation	1.44	3.6	41.9
Factor 8	Beliefs about failure	1.39	3.4	45.3
Factor 9	Enjoyment	1.28	3.0	48.3

Fourteen items load on Factor 1:

	Loading
I plan to continue studying English for as long as possible.	.71
My attendance in this class will be good.	.71
If I do well in this course, it will be because I try hard.	.64
This English class will definitely help me improve my English.	.63
After I finish this class, I will probably take another English course.	.62
I really want to learn more English in this class than I have in the past.	.61
I often think about how to learn English better.	.58
I expect to do well in this class because I am good at learning English.	.54
If I don't do well in this class, it will be because I don't try hard enough.	.52
I can honestly say that I really put my best effort into trying to learn English.	.52
My relationship with the teacher in this class is important to me.	.49
I am learning English to become more educated.	.49
English is important to me because it will broaden my view.	.49
If the fees for this class were increased, I would still enroll because studying English is important to me.	.47

The items loading highest on the first factor can be divided into three categories: those asserting high motivational strength and determination to learn English well (seven items: *plan to continue; attendance will be good; will probably take another course; want to learn more than in the past; think about how to learn English better; I can honestly say that I really put my best effort into trying to learn English; would still enroll if fees increased*); items concerning expectations of success (four items: *class will definitely help improve English; if I do well in this course, it will be because I try hard; expect to do well in this class because good at learning English; if I don't do well in this class it will be because I don't try hard enough*); plus three more heterogeneous items (*relationship with teacher is important; I am learning English to become more educated; English is important to me because it will broaden my view*). It is interesting to note that the four items from the expectancy/control subsection of the motivational questionnaire that load on Factor 1 all attribute success or failure to ability or effort, rather than external causes (the teacher, task difficulty). This factor might be labeled "expectation of success," but it seems to us even stronger than that, and we have called it "determination."

Factor 2 is readily interpretable, since it consists of all the items from the anxiety subscale of the motivational questionnaire:

	Loading
I feel uncomfortable if I have to speak in my English class.	.81
It embarrasses me to volunteer answers in my English class.	.80

I don't like to speak often in English class because I am afraid that my   .80
teacher will think I am not a good student.

I'm afraid other students will laugh at me when I speak English.   .61

I think I can learn English well, but I don't perform well on tests and   .46
examinations.

I often have difficulty concentrating in English class.   .46

It is interesting that difficulty in concentrating in class loads on this factor, suggesting that concentration is not a purely cognitive variable. Many psychologists relate anxiety to the intrusion of unwelcome thoughts and difficulty in concentrating.

Factor 3 consists of four questionnaire items, all from the extrinsic motivation subscale of the questionnaire, all with a strong instrumental orientation:

	Loading
Being able to speak English will add to my social status.	.75
If I learn English better, I will be able to get a better job.	.71
Increasing my English proficiency will have financial benefits for me.	.61
If I can speak English, I will have a marvelous life.	.48

Factor 4 consists of three questionnaire items, all addressing personal needs for affiliation. We have labeled the dimension "sociability." The items loading on this factor concern the classroom as a social environment and a concern with getting along with both students (as potential friends) and the teacher.

	Loading
One reason I learn English is that I can meet new people and make friends in class.	.67
My relationship with the teacher in this class is important to me.	.60
One of the most important things in this class is getting along with other students.	.52

Factor 5 consists of four items concerning target language speakers and American and British culture. We label this factor "attitudes toward foreign culture." This factor might also be considered to represent an integrative orientation.

	Loading
The English are conservative people who cherish customs and traditions.	.71
Americans are very friendly people.	.64
Most of my favorite actors and musicians are either British or American.	.61
British culture has contributed a lot to the world.	.46

Factor 6 consists of only two items, and we have labeled it "foreign residence."

	Loading
I am learning English because I want to spend time in an English-speaking country.	.72
I want to learn English because I would like to emigrate.	.61

Factor 7 consists of three questionnaire items from the intrinsic motivation subscale:

	Loading
Learning English is a hobby for me.	.65
I don't enjoy learning English, but I know that learning English is important for me. (reverse-coded)	.57
I wish I could learn English in an easier way, without going to class. (reverse-coded)	.47

The two items that load on Factor 8 concern beliefs about failure, specifically the attribution of failure to external causes:

	Loading
If I don't learn well in this class, it will be mainly because of the teacher.	.71
If I don't do well in this class, it will be because the class is too difficult.	.71

Factor 9 is labeled "enjoyment" after the single item loading on it, although conceptually there is little to distinguish it from the items loading on Factor 7 (intrinsic motivation):

	Loading
I enjoy learning English very much.	.51

FACTOR ANALYSIS OF INSTRUCTIONAL PREFERENCES

For the factor analysis of our informants' preferences for classroom activities and methodological approaches, a six-factor solution was chosen based on the same criteria mentioned above with respect to the factor analysis of the motivation questionnaire. This solution accounts for 50.3% of the total variance, as indicated in Table 4.

Table 4: Factor analysis for Part B: Preferences for instructional activities

	Label	Eigenvalue	Variance	Cumulative variance
Factor 1	Balanced approach	3.57	12.7	12.7
Factor 2	Group & pair work	1.26	8.6	21.3
Factor 3	Silent learner	2.72	8.5	29.6
Factor 4	Challenge/ curiosity	1.41	8.2	38
Factor 5	Direct method	1.02	6.9	45
Factor 6	Feedback	1.1	5.4	50.3

Six questionnaire items load on Factor 1:

	Loading
It is important for the teacher to maintain discipline in English class.	.71
Students in English class should let the teacher know why they are studying English so that the lessons can be made relevant to their goals.	.67
Student should ask questions whenever they have not understood a point in class.	.65
Reading and writing should be emphasized in English class.	.64
Listening and speaking should be emphasized in English class.	.47
Activities in this class should be designed to help the students improve their abilities to communicate in English.	.46

The items loading on this factor concern two different aspects of the language classroom, the contrast between teacher-fronted and student-centered classrooms, and the skill areas to be emphasized. It seems that subjects scoring high on this factor prefer a balanced approach with respect to both of these aspects. The teacher is to be in control to the extent of maintaining classroom discipline, but students should ask questions when they do not understand a point made in class and should make their reasons for learning English known so that lessons can be made relevant to their goals. All four skill areas (listening, speaking, reading, writing) should be emphasized (questionnaire items concerning pronunciation and grammar did not load on this factor), and the goal of the class should be to improve the learners' communicative ability. We label this factor "the balanced approach."

Factor 2 contains three items concerning individualistic and cooperative learning situations, specifically, attitudes toward group and pair work:

	Loading
I like English learning activities in which students work together in pairs or small groups.	.79
I prefer to work by myself in English class, not with other students.	−.75
Group activities and pair work in English class are a waste of time.	−.68

A positive score on this factor means that an individual likes cooperative learning structures. A negative score on the factor means that an individual does not like group activities or pair work, thinks they are a waste of time, and would rather work alone.

Factor 3 contains four items that seem somewhat similar to those of Factor 2 in their anti-communicative bias, though in this case, the issue is not individualism versus cooperation but talking or remaining silent. We label this factor "the silent learner," to reflect the items that load on it:

	Loading
In English class, the teacher should do most of the talking and students should only answer.	.67
Pronunciation should not be an important focus of the English class.	.60
Communication activities are a waste of time in this class, because I only need to learn what is necessary to pass English examinations.	.57
I prefer to sit and listen, and don't like being forced to speak in English class.	.57

Factor 4 is labeled "challenge and curiosity" after the first two items that load on it:

	Loading
In a class like this, I prefer activities and materials that really challenge me so that I can learn more.	.81
In an English class, I prefer activities and materials that arouse my curiosity even if they are difficult to learn.	.79
I prefer an English class with lots of activities that allow active participation.	.46

Factor 5 consists of only two items:

	Loading
During English class, I would like to have only English spoken.	.76
English class is most useful when the emphasis is put on grammar.	−.58

The two items loading on Factor 5 are negatively correlated with each other. Those who score high on the factor think that only the target language should be used and do not think that grammatical explanations should be emphasized. Those who score low on this factor do want grammar emphasized and do not think the target language needs to be used all the time. These are the most basic points of contrast between traditional grammar-translation approaches to foreign language teaching and various "direct" methods (including the natural approach in the US and communicative language teaching internationally), so we have labeled this factor "direct method."

Factor 6 is labeled "feedback." Only two items load on it:

	Loading
It is important that the teacher give immediate feedback in class so that students know whether their responses are right or wrong.	.80
The teacher should not criticize students who make mistakes in class.	.53

FACTOR ANALYSIS OF LEARNING STRATEGIES

For the factor analysis of our subjects' statements concerning the cognitive strategies that are most typical of their learning behavior, a five-factor solution was chosen based on the same criteria mentioned above with respect to the factor analyses of the motivation and classroom preferences questionnaires. This solution accounts for 47.30% of the total variance, as shown in Table 5.

Table 5: Factor analysis for Part C: Learning strategies

	Label	Eigenvalue	Variance	Cumulative variance
Factor 1	Active involvement	6.82	17.08	17.08
Factor 2	Organizing learning	1.52	11.49	28.58
Factor 3	Resource mgmnt	1.25	7.56	36.14
Factor 4	Coping strategies	1.17	6.09	42.23
Factor 5	Time mgmnt	1.07	5.07	47.3

Factor 1 is labeled "active involvement." The eight questionnaire items that load on this factor represent a variety of learning strategies, including rehearsal, inferencing, self-monitoring, and calling upon others for help:

	Loading
When I read something in English, I usually read it more than once.	.70
I say or write new expressions in English repeatedly in order to practice them.	.66
I always go back over a test to make sure I understand everything.	.64
I always try to evaluate my progress in learning English.	.62
When studying for a test, I try to determine which concepts I don't understand well.	.61
I learn from my mistakes in using English by trying to understand the reasons for them.	.61
Whenever I have a question, I ask my teacher about it or try to find the answer in another way.	.60
I actively look for people with whom I can speak English.	.50

Factor 2 is labeled "organizing learning." It consists of five items representing the learning strategies of elaboration and organization and a generally analytic style of learning:

	Loading
I always try to notice the similarities and differences between English and Arabic.	.70
When I learn a new grammar rule, I think about its relationship to rules I have learned already.	.69
When I study for my English course, I pick out the most important points and make charts, diagrams, and tables for myself.	.55
I make summaries of what I have learned in my English class.	.55
I try to find the meaning of a word by dividing it into parts that I understand.	.46

Factor 3 is labeled "resource management." It consists of two items dealing with arranging a time and place to study English:

	Loading
I have a regular place set aside for studying.	.75
I arrange my schedule to make sure that I keep up with my English class.	.70

Factor 4 is labeled "coping strategies." It consists of three items: memorization (rehearsal), guessing from context, and inferencing.

	Loading
When learning new English words, I say them over and over to memorize them.	.63

	Loading
When I do not understand a word in something I am reading, I try to guess its meaning from context.	.56
I try to look for patterns in English without waiting for the teacher to explain the rules to me.	.53

Factor 5 is labeled "time management." It consists of two items, both reflecting time pressures and the need to be efficient:

	Loading
I often find that I don't spend much time studying English because of other activities.	.63
When studying for a test, first I think about what the most important points are, instead of just reading everything over.	.45

MULTIDIMENSIONAL SCALING

Factor analysis is by far the preferred method of analysis in studies of language learning motivation (O'Bryen, 1995). Although the factor analyses presented so far have a certain amount of face validity and are comparable in many respects to other studies of foreign language learning motivation, there are several reasons these results are not as satisfactory as might be hoped. The combined variance accounted for by the three factor analyses is no greater than 50% for any of the three analyses. This means that an unspecified number of factors other than the nine we identified for the motivational questionnaire also accounted for about 50% of the variance. One reason for this might be that our scales were not interval (evenly spaced), which is an assumption of factor analysis, but not of multidimensional scaling (Hatch and Lazaraton, 1991). We therefore proceeded to carry out multidimensional scaling on the same data.

This statistical tool, which has rarely been used in any area of second and foreign language studies, is related to factor analysis in that it is also a data reduction model, a set of mathematical techniques that enables researchers to uncover the hidden structure of a data set (Kruskal and Wish, 1978). It differs from factor analysis in that it can usually fit an appropriate model into fewer dimensions, and unlike factor analysis, which is linear, MDS is a spatial model. A set of data is represented by a set of points in a spatial configuration or map. Each axis of the map represents a dimension. Whereas in factor analysis only a small set of items typically loads on a particular factor, in MDS each item is located somewhere along the continuum indicated by each dimension (much as a collection of people could be placed into a three-dimensional space defined by dimensions of age, height, and weight). By finding key differences between items at opposite ends of each dimension, the theoretical meaning of the analysis can be determined.

MULTIDIMENSIONAL SCALING OF THE MOTIVATION QUESTIONNAIRE

Multidimensional scaling of the 50 items of the motivation questionnaire indicated that 85% of the variance could be accounted for with a three-dimensional model

---

(stress of final configuration = 0.147). Spatially, certain clusters of items occupy a distinctive space in the model. For example, those questionnaire items related to anxiety fell into a cluster defined by low values on the first dimension, moderately high on the second dimension, and low on the third dimension (the analysis of such clusters is similar to factor analysis).

Tables 6, 7, and 8 show the distribution of all questionnaire items along the three dimensions.

Table 6: Motivation Dimension 1 (Affect)

I don't enjoy learning English, but I know that learning English is important for me. (reverse-coded)	1.64
I wish I could learn English in an easier way, without going to class. (reversed)	1.60
I enjoy learning English very much.	1.01
Learning English is a hobby for me.	.88
I expect to do well in this class because I am good at learning English.	.87
Learning English is a challenge that I enjoy.	.81
The English are conservative people who cherish customs and traditions.	.71
My attendance in this class will be good.	.68
I really want to learn more English in this class than I have done in the past.	.66
I plan to continue studying English for as long as possible.	.65
English is important to me because it will broaden my view.	.63
British culture has contributed a lot to the world.	.56
After I finish this class, I will probably take another English course.	.47
I can honestly say that I really put my best effort into trying to learn English.	.46
Americans are very friendly people.	.43
Most of my favorite actors and musicians are either British or American.	.37
If the fees for this class were increased, I would still enroll because studying English is important to me.	.37
My relationship with the teacher in this class is important to me.	.33
Everybody in Egypt should be able to speak English.	.32

I want to learn English because it is useful when traveling in many countries.	.30
This English class will definitely help me improve my English.	.30
It is important to me to do better than the other students in my class.	.29
If I do well in this course, it will be because I try hard.	.28
I am learning English to become more educated.	.24
I need to be able to read textbooks in English.	.23
If I don't do well in this class, it will be because I don't try hard enough.	.23
I often think about how I can learn English better.	.12
If I can speak English, I will have a marvelous life.	.01
One of the most important things in this class is getting along with the other students.	−.06
This class is important to me because if I learn English well, I will be able to help my children learn English.	−.15
If I learn a lot in this class, it will be because of the teacher.	−.05
Being able to speak English will add to my social status.	−.07
I am learning English because I want to spend a period of time in an English-speaking country.	−.14
If I learn English better, I will be able to get a better job.	−.19
Increasing my English proficiency will have financial benefits for me.	−.20
I want to learn English because I would like to emigrate.	−.25
If I don't do well in this class, it will be because I don't have much ability for learning English.	−.52
One reason I learn English is that I can meet new people and make friends in my English class.	−.57
I want to do well in this class because it is important to show my ability to my family/friends/supervisors/others.	−.65
If I don't learn well in this class, it will be mainly because of the teacher.	−.71
If I do well in this class, it will be because this is an easy class.	−.84
The main reason I am taking this class is that my parents/my spouse/my supervisors want me to improve my English.	−1.00
The main reason I need to learn English is to pass examinations.	−1.04

continued...

Table 6: Motivation Dimension 1 (Affect) (cont.)

If I don't do well in this class, it will be because the class is too difficult.	−1.08
I think I can learn English well, but I don't perform well on tests and examinations.	−1.18
I often have difficulty concentrating in English class.	−1.23
I don't like to speak often in English class because I am afraid my teacher will think I am not a good student.	−1.29
I am afraid other students will laugh at me when I speak English.	−1.38
I feel uncomfortable if I have to speak in my English class.	−1.41
It embarrasses me to volunteer answers in my English class.	−1.43

Table 7: Motivation Dimension 2 (Goal Orientation)

After I finish this class, I will probably take another English course.	.85
I often think about how I can learn English better.	.75
If the fees for this class were increased, I would still enroll because studying English is important to me.	.73
If I learn a lot in this class, it will be because of the teacher.	.56
If I don't do well in this class, it will be because I don't try hard enough.	.53
I plan to continue studying English for as long as possible.	.48
It embarrasses me to volunteer answers in my English class.	.46
I often have difficulty concentrating in English class.	.45
My attendance in this class will be good.	.44
I can honestly say that I really put my best effort into trying to learn English.	.40
I don't like to speak often in English class because I am afraid that my teacher will think I am not a good student.	.39
This class is important to me because if I learn English well, I will be able to help my children learn English.	.36
I wish I could learn English in an easier way, without going to class. (reversed)	.36
This English class will definitely help me improve my English.	.33
I feel uncomfortable if I have to speak in my English class.	.31
I don't do well in this class, it will be because I don't have much ability for learning English.	.29
If I do well in this course, it will be because I try hard.	.28
I am learning English to become more educated.	.26
My relationship with the teacher in this class is important to me.	.25
I really want to learn more English in this class than I have done in the past.	.21

One of the most important things in this class is getting along with other students.	.17
I am afraid other students will laugh at me when I speak English.	.13
I enjoy learning English very much.	.13
I think I can learn English well, but I don't perform well on tests and examinations.	.10
English is important to me because it will broaden my view.	.06
It is important to me to do better than the other students in my class.	.04
Learning English is a hobby for me.	−.01
Learning English is a challenge that I enjoy.	−.03
I don't enjoy learning English, but I know that learning English is important for me. (reverse-coded)	−.03
If I don't do well in this class, it will be because the class is too difficult.	−.04
If I can speak English, I will have a marvelous life.	−.07
If I do well in this class, it will be because this is an easy class.	−.10
Being able to speak English will add to my social status.	−.11
Everybody in Egypt should be able to speak English.	−.12
I want to do well in this class because it is important to show my ability to my family/friends/supervisors/others.	−.15
I expect to do well in this class because I am good at learning English.	−.22
The main reason I am taking this class is that my parents/my spouse/my supervisors want me to improve my English.	−.30
I want to learn English because it is useful when traveling in many countries.	−.31
If I learn English better, I will be able to get a better job.	−.35
Americans are very friendly people.	−.36
If I don't learn well in this class, it will be mainly because of the teacher.	−.38
The main reason I need to learn English is to pass examinations.	−.41
One reason I learn English is that I can meet new people and make friends in my English class.	−.53
I need to be able to read textbooks in English.	−.62
I am learning English because I want to spend a period of time in an English-speaking country.	−.63
Increasing my English proficiency will have financial benefits for me.	−.75
Most of my favorite actors and musicians are either British or American.	−.85
British culture has contributed a lot to the world.	−.91
I want to learn English because I would like to emigrate.	−1.00
The English are conservative people who cherish customs and traditions.	−1.07

Table 8: Motivation Dimension 3 (Expectancy)

Increasing my English proficiency will have financial benefits for me.	.74
If I learn English better, I will be able to get a better job.	.71
I need to be able to read textbooks in English.	.71
It is important to me to do better than the other students in my class.	.69
One of the most important things in this class is getting along with other students.	.52
I am learning English to become more educated.	.52
I want to do well in this class because it is important to show my ability to my family/friends/supervisors/others.	.49
I really want to learn more English in this class than I have done in the past.	.48
This class is important to me because if I learn English well, I will be able to help my children learn English.	.48
Being able to speak English will add to my social status.	.46
My relationship with the teacher in this class is important to me.	.43
I want to learn English because it is useful when traveling in many countries.	.39
The main reason I am taking this class is that my parents/my spouse/my supervisors want me to improve my English.	.38
One reason I learn English is that I can meet new people and make friends in my English class.	.34
I often think about how I can learn English better.	.33
Everybody in Egypt should be able to speak English.	.32
English is important to me because it will broaden my view.	.32
This English class will definitely help me improve my English.	.26
I often have difficulty concentrating in English class.	.16
I am learning English because I want to spend a period of time in an English-speaking country.	.15
If I can speak English, I will have a marvelous life.	.15
My attendance in this class will be good.	.13
After I finish this class, I will probably take another English course.	.13
If I do well in this course, it will be because I try hard.	.12
I plan to continue studying English for as long as possible.	.07
I expect to do well in this class because I am good at learning English.	.05
The main reason I need to learn English is to pass examinations.	.02
I can honestly say that I really put my best effort into trying to learn English.	−.02
I enjoy learning English very much.	−.06
I want to learn English because I would like to emigrate.	−.09
Learning English is a challenge that I enjoy.	−.11
I don't like to speak often in English class because I am afraid that my teacher will think I am not a good student.	−.14

If I learn a lot in this class, it will be because of the teacher.	−.15
I think I can learn English well, but I don't perform well on tests and examinations.	−.17
I feel uncomfortable if I have to speak in my English class.	−.26
It embarrasses me to volunteer answers in my English class.	−.27
I am afraid other students will laugh at me when I speak English.	−.28
If I do well in this class, it will be because this is an easy class.	−.31
British culture has contributed a lot to the world.	−.36
Most of my favorite actors and musicians are either British or American.	−.38
Americans are very friendly people.	−.39
If the fees for this class were increased, I would still enroll because studying English is important to me.	−.40
I wish I could learn English in an easier way, without going to class. (reversed)	−.43
The English are conservative people who cherish customs and traditions.	−.71
Learning English is a hobby for me.	−.72
If I don't do well in this class, it will be because the class is too difficult.	−.77
I don't enjoy learning English, but I know that learning English is important for me. (reverse-coded)	−.77
If I don't do well in this class, it will be because I don't try hard enough.	−.80
If I don't do well in this class, it will be because I don't have much ability for learning English.	−.85
If I don't learn well in this class, it will be mainly because of the teacher.	−1.13

We have labeled Dimension 1 "affect." Alternatively, it could be labeled "enjoyment" or "intrinsic motivation." The distribution of items along this dimension supports Csikszentmihalyi's model of intrinsic motivation (Csikszentmihalyi and Nakamura, 1989; Wong and Csikszentmihalyi, 1991). At one end of the continuum, we find what Csikszentmihalyi calls "flow," the self-motivating feeling of enjoyment (*I enjoy learning English very much*) that one experiences in association with both challenge (*learning English is a challenge that I enjoy*) and skill (*I expect to do well in this class because I'm good at learning English*). At the other end of the continuum represented by Dimension 1 are found items relating to high challenge (*I want to do well in this class because it is important to show my ability to my family/friends/supervisors/others*) coupled with low skill (*I think I can learn English well, but I don't perform well on tests and examinations*), which in Csikszentmihalyi's theory results in anxiety (*it embarrasses me to volunteer answers in my English class; I feel uncomfortable if I have to speak in my English class*), the opposite of flow. In this case, there may be extrinsic motivation (*the main reason I need to learn English is to pass exams*), but the enjoyment and cognitive efficiency are impaired (*I often have difficulty concentrating in English class*).

Motivation Dimension 2 is much harder to interpret. After much thought and discussion, we have labeled this dimension "goal orientation," but other labels might be "internal" versus "external" reference, a "learning" versus "performance" orientation, or "extrinsic motivation." The key to interpreting this dimension appears to be the negative end of the continuum, where most questionnaire items concerning extrinsic motivation for learning English are found. There is a lot of variety in the items represented (*I want to learn English because I would like to emigrate; increasing my English proficiency will have financial benefits for me; I need to be able to read textbooks in English; if I learn English better, I will be able to get a better job*), and integratively oriented items also fall toward the same end of this dimension (*most of my favorite actors and musicians are either British or American; one reason I learn English is that I can meet new people and make friends in my English class*). But, all of these items represent "reasons" for studying English. At the other end of the continuum are items that might be characterized as learning English for no particular reason, i.e., sources of motivation unrelated to external reasons or rewards. The two items from the extrinsic motivation subscale that are at the positive end of Dimension 2 (*English is important to me because it will broaden my view; I am learning English to become more educated*) seem similar to other items at the positive end because they stress internal rather than external sources of reward. We also note that all items concerning anxiety are fairly high on this dimension. This suggests that those who are motivated by internal goals may be more anxious than those who have concrete, external goals.

Dimension 3 is labeled "expectancy." Once again, a number of other labels might be appropriate, including "success orientation," "determination," "confidence," "positive thinking," or even "denial." What is most striking to us about Dimension 3 is that many of the items that load at the positive end of the dimension are expressed in a very positive way (*increasing my English proficiency will have financial benefits for me; if I learn English better, I will be able to get a better job; this class is important to me because if I learn English well, I will be able to help my children learn English; being able to speak English will add to my social status*). Qualified statements of success (*if I do well in this course, it will be because...*) fall in the middle of the continuum. At the extreme negative end of the dimension are all four questionnaire items concerning attributions of failure (*if I don't do well in this class, it will be because...*). It seems as though it does not matter much which attribution statement is presented for response; if failure is mentioned, the item falls at the negative pole of this dimension.

MULTIDIMENSIONAL SCALING OF INSTRUCTIONAL PREFERENCES

Multidimensional scaling of the 22 items in Part B of the questionnaire (preferences for instructional activities) indicated that 88% of the variance could be accounted for with a two-dimensional model (stress of final configuration = 0.12). Tables 9 and 10 show the distribution of all questionnaire items along the two dimensions.

Table 9: Instructional Preferences Dimension 1 (Communicative Orientation)

I prefer an English class in which there are lots of activities that allow me to participate actively.	1.19
Activities in this class should be designed to help the students improve their abilities to communicate in English.	1.10
I like English learning activities in which students work together in pairs or small groups.	1.02
In English class, the teacher should do most of the talking and the students should only answer when they are called upon.	−.84
Listening and speaking should be emphasized in English class.	.78
It is important that the teacher give immediate feedback in class so that students know whether their responses are right or wrong.	.78
Student should ask questions whenever they have not understood a point in class.	.74
In an English class, I prefer activities and materials that arouse my curiosity even if they are difficult to learn.	.67
During English class, I would like to have only English spoken.	.66
In a class like this, I prefer activities and materials that really challenge me so that I can learn more.	.57
It is important for the teacher to maintain discipline in English class.	.46
Students in English class should let the teacher know why they are studying English so that the lessons can be made relevant to their goals.	.27
The teacher should make sure that everyone in this class learns English equally well.	.30
Reading and writing should be emphasized in English class.	.02
The teacher should not criticize students who make mistakes in class.	−.32
English class is most useful when the emphasis is put on grammar.	−.48
In my English class, the teacher should explain things in Arabic sometimes in order to help us learn.	−.68
I prefer to sit and listen, and don't like being forced to speak in English class.	−1.16
I prefer to work by myself in English class, not with other students.	−1.18
Communication activities are a waste of time in this class, because I only need to learn what is necessary to pass English examinations.	−1.28
Group activities and pair work in English class are a waste of time.	−1.29
Pronunciation should not be an important focus of the English class.	−1.36

Table 10: Instructional Preferences Dimension 2 (Teacher Control)

In my English class, the teacher should explain things in Arabic sometimes in order to help us learn.	.69
It is important for the teacher to maintain discipline in English class.	.52
The teacher should make sure that everyone in this class learns English equally well.	.51
Reading and writing should be emphasized in English class.	.47
Student should ask questions whenever they have not understood a point in class.	.44
I like English learning activities in which students work together in pairs or small groups.	.38
English class is most useful when the emphasis is put on grammar.	.36
I prefer to sit and listen, and don't like being forced to speak in English class.	.33
It is important that the teacher give immediate feedback in class so that students know whether their responses are right or wrong.	.23
In English class, the teacher should do most of the talking and the students should only answer when they are called upon.	.17
Communication activities are a waste of time in this class, because I only need to learn what is necessary to pass English examinations.	.11
Students in English class should let the teacher know why they are studying English so that the lessons can be made relevant to their goals.	.11
Listening and speaking should be emphasized in English class.	.06
Activities in this class should be designed to help the students improve their abilities to communicate in English.	−.05
Pronunciation should not be an important focus of the English class.	−.07
I prefer an English class in which there are lots of activities that allow me to participate actively.	−.23
In a class like this, I prefer activities and materials that really challenge me so that I can learn more.	−.24
I prefer to work by myself in English class, not with other students.	−.40
In an English class, I prefer activities and materials that arouse my curiosity even if they are difficult to learn.	−.47
Group activities and pair work in English class are a waste of time.	−.50
The teacher should not criticize students who make mistakes in class.	−1.09
During English class, I would like to have only English spoken.	−1.31

Dimension 1 represents a communicative orientation. Items that concern active participation and activities designed to help students improve their ability to communicate, such as small group and pair work, are at the positive end of this dimension. Statements that dismiss communicative activities while welcoming a focus on grammar and explanations in Arabic are at the negative end of the dimension.

Dimension 2 is labeled "teacher control." Most questionnaire items that even mention the teacher are at the positive end of this dimension: the teacher should maintain discipline, explain as necessary, and be responsible for student learning.

MULTIDIMENSIONAL SCALING OF LEARNING STRATEGIES

Multidimensional scaling of the 25 items in Part C of the questionnaire (learning strategies) indicated that 81% of the variance could be accounted for with a two-dimensional model (stress of final configuration = 0.19). Tables 11 and 12 show the distribution of all questionnaire items along the two dimensions.

Table 11: Strategy Dimension 1 (Traditional Orientation)

I always try to memorize grammar rules.	1.29
I always arrange time to prepare before every English class.	.86
I always try to notice the similarities and differences between English and Arabic.	.71
When learning new English words, I say them over and over to memorize them.	.68
I make summaries of what I have learned in my English class.	.68
I try to change the way I study in order to fit the teacher's teaching style.	.66
When I study for my English course, I pick out the most important points and make charts, diagrams, and tables for myself.	.63
I say or write new expressions in English repeatedly to practice them.	.58
When I learn a new grammar rule, I think about its relationship to rules I have learned already.	.31
When I don't do well on a test, I go back over it to make sure I understand everything.	.24
I arrange my schedule to make sure that I keep up with my English class.	.24
When I read something in English, I usually read it more than once.	.20
I have a regular place set aside for studying.	.08
I always try to evaluate my progress in learning English.	−.01
When studying for a test, I try to determine which concepts I don't understand well.	−.02
When I learn a new word in English, I try to relate it to other English words I know.	−.09
I try to find the meaning of a word by dividing it into parts that I understand.	−.17

continued...

Table 11: Strategy Dimension 1 (Traditional Orientation) (cont.)

Whenever I have a question, I ask my teacher about it or try to find the answer in another way.	−.19
I learn from my mistakes in using English by trying to understand the reasons for them.	−.26
I actively look for people with whom I can speak English.	−.36
When preparing my English lessons, I read the material through first to get a general idea of what it is about and what the major points are.	−.47
I try to look for patterns in English without waiting for the teacher to explain the rules to me.	−.67
When studying for a test, I think about the most important points.	−.98
When I do not understand a word in something I am reading, I try to guess its meaning from context.	−1.39
I often find that I don't spend much time studying English because of other activities.	−2.56

Table 12: Strategy Dimension 2 (Internal versus External Resources)

When studying for a test, I think about the most important points.	1.65
I always try to notice the similarities and differences between English and Arabic.	1.07
I try to find the meaning of a word by dividing it into parts that I understand.	.73
I try to change the way I study in order to fit the teacher's teaching style.	.63
When I learn a new grammar rule, I think about its relationship to rules I have learned already.	.45
When I do not understand a word in something I am reading, I try to guess its meaning from context.	.31
When I learn a new word in English, I try to relate it to other English words I know.	.30
When I study for my English course, I pick out the most important points and make charts, diagrams, and tables for myself.	.25
I try to look for patterns in English without waiting for the teacher to explain the rules to me.	.13
I make summaries of what I have learned in my English class.	.11
I always try to memorize grammar rules.	.01
I always try to evaluate my progress in learning English.	.03
When studying for a test, I try to determine which concepts I don't understand well.	.00
I learn from my mistakes in using English by trying to understand the reasons for them.	−.05
When I read something in English, I usually read it more than once.	−.13

When preparing my English lessons, I read the material through first to get a general idea of what it is about and what the major points are.	–.21
I say or write new expressions in English repeatedly to practice them.	–.27
When I don't do well on a test, I go back over it to make sure I understand everything.	–.30
When learning new English words, I say them over and over to memorize them.	–.38
Whenever I have a question, I ask my teacher about it or try to find the answer in another way.	–.46
I always arrange time to prepare before every English class.	–.54
I often find that I don't spend much time studying English because of other activities.	–.59
I arrange my schedule to make sure that I keep up with my English class.	–.64
I actively look for people with whom I can speak English.	–.72
I have a regular place set aside for studying.	–1.39

Dimension 1 has been labeled "traditional orientation." At the positive end of this dimension we find a number of items that resemble "learning," as contrasted with "acquisition" in Krashen's sense (Krashen, 1981), e.g., *I always try to memorize grammar rules; I always try to notice the similarities and differences between English and Arabic; I make summaries of what I have learned in my English class*. Those at the negative end of this dimension represent a more relaxed style, less focused on study and conscious rule learning, e.g., *when I do not understand a word in something I am reading, I try to guess its meaning from context; when preparing my English lessons, I read the material through first to get a general idea of what it is about and what the major points are; I actively look for people with whom I can speak English*.

We have labeled Dimension 2 "internal versus external resources." At the negative end are items concerned with place (*I have a regular place set aside for studying*), time (*I arrange my schedule to make sure I keep up with my English class; I always arrange time to prepare*), and people (*when I have a question, I ask my teacher; I actively look for people with whom I can speak English*). Items falling at the positive end of this dimension concern the learner's own internal resources (e.g., *I think about the most important point; I try to notice similarities and differences; I try to find the meaning of a word by dividing it into parts that I understand*).

MOTIVATION, LEARNING STRATEGIES, AND INSTRUCTIONAL PREFERENCES

In order to identify relationships between motivation and the other two foci of this study, instructional preferences and learning strategies, Pearson correlation matrices were set up using both factors identified through the factor analysis and the dimensions identified through multidimensional scaling.

Using the results of factor analysis as input, the following significant correlations were found:

Motivation F1 (Determination)

Preferences F1 (Balanced approach)	.454
Preferences F4 (Challenge/curiosity)	.309
Strategies F1 (Active involvement)	.583
Strategies F2 (Organizing learning)	.376
Strategies F3 (Resource management)	.332
Strategies F4 (Coping strategies)	.388

Motivation F2 (Anxiety)

Preferences F3 (The silent learner)	.397

Motivation F3 (Instrumental)

Strategies F1 (Active involvement)	.267

Motivation F4 (Sociability)

Strategies F1 (Active involvement)	.280

Motivation F4 (Sociability)

Strategies F2 (Organizing learning)	.290

These results indicate that, for this sample of adult EFL students, determined learners who expect to succeed prefer a balanced approach in the foreign language classroom, appreciate challenging tasks and activities that arouse their curiosity, even if they are difficult, and are more likely to report that they use learning strategies of nearly all types than are less determined learners. Like determined learners, students who score high on instrumental motivation as well as those who rate high on the motivational factor of sociability are also active learners. Like determined learners, students high in sociability also organize their own learning. Students who score high on the anxiety factor, on the other hand, would rather not participate actively in class but prefer to be silent, and anxiety is not significantly associated with any set of learning strategies. Although an integrative orientation does emerge from these data and in spite of the fact that integrativeness has been associated with active learning in other studies (Gardner, 1985b, 1988), integrativeness in our data did not correlate significantly with any set of instructional preferences or learning strategies.

Using the results of the multidimensional scaling analysis as input, only two significant correlations were found:

Motivation D1 (Affect)

Preferences D1 (Communicative)   .46

Strategies D1 (Traditional orientation)

Preferences D2 (Teacher control)   .42

Students who scored high on affect, indicating enjoyment of the process of learning, indicated a preference for activities that allow them to participate actively and will help them to improve their ability to communicate, including group and pair work. Students who scored low in enjoyment and high in anxiety rejected group activities, pair work, and other communicative activities as a waste of time and prefer to be silent and work alone. Students with a traditional orientation to learning (memorizing grammar rules, making comparisons between English and Arabic) indicated a preference for classes in which the teacher maintains control and guides learning. Students with a less traditional, more relaxed attitude toward language learning were less concerned with what teachers do to structure their learning and the classroom environment.

MOTIVATION, AGE, GENDER, AND PROFICIENCY

Data were collected concerning a number of background variables for all informants. Preliminary analyses indicated that the three variables of age, gender, and English language proficiency (as indicated by class placement) were the most interesting in terms of their relationships to our informants' motivational profiles. Because of space limitations, only those three independent variables are being reported, and only with respect to the dimensions of motivation derived through multidimensional scaling as dependent variables.

Table 13 shows the means for each of the three dimensions of motivation for each background category. Table 14 shows the results of three three-way ANOVAs for each of the dimensions using the independent variables of age, proficiency and gender. Because three different ANOVAs were carried out, alpha was set at .017 for each measure in order to preserve an overall level of .05 for the analysis as a whole.

Table 13: Background variables and means on dimensions of motivation

| | | MEANS | | |
	N	D1 (Affect)	D2 (Goals)	D3 (Expectancy)
Age:				
15–18	69	30.030	6.287	11.273
19–22	347	28.959	7.298	9.443
23–35	840	30.860	6.328	9.685
35+	192	32.257	7.198	8.208
Proficiency:				
Basic	208	25.411	9.187	10.198
Elemen.	359	27.295	7.034	9.762
Low int.	302	30.134	6.346	10.249
Intermed.	230	33.500	5.944	9.422
Upper int.	205	33.474	6.023	8.798
Advanced	160	36.380	4.955	7.789
Gender:				
Males	792	31.034	5.370	9.888
Females	672	29.746	8.173	9.101

Table 14: Results of ANOVAs with repeated measures on each of the dimensions of motivation

	F-ratio	P
Dimension 1 (Affect)		
N = 1447, Multiple R = 0.292, R squared = 0.085, Error = 205.335		
Age	0.363	0.78
Proficiency	12.627	0.00*
Sex	1.268	0.25
Age*Proficiency	1.012	0.439

Age*Sex	1.396	0.242
Proficiency*Sex	1.713	0.128
Age*Proficiency*Sex	0.623	0.858
Dimension 2 (Goals)		
N = 1447, Multiple R = 0.363, R squared = 0.132, Error = 34.410		
Age	1.95	0.12
Proficiency	5.272	0.00*
Sex	37.742	0.00*
Age*Proficiency	1.557	0.079
Age*Sex	1.378	0.248
Proficiency*Sex	1.473	0.196
Age*Proficiency*Sex	1.553	0.080
Dimension 3 (Expectancy)		
N = 1447, Multiple R = 0.241, R squared = 0.058, Error = 37.491		
Age	7.623	0.00*
Proficiency	2.78	0.017*
Sex	5.544	0.019
Age*Proficiency	1.186	0.275
Age*Sex	1.638	0.179
Proficiency*Sex	1.38	0.229
Age*Proficiency*Sex	1.024	0.427

With respect to motivation Dimension 1, enjoyment of learning English, Table 14 indicates that a main effect was found only for language proficiency (p = 0.00). Advanced learners enjoy English class the most; basic level students enjoy learning English the least and are the most anxious. Both Scheffé and Tukey post-hoc tests showed that proficiency level 1 (basic) was significantly different on this measure from each of the other groups (p = .01). As can be seen in Table 13, differences on Dimension 1 with respect to age and gender are inconsistent, and as indicated in Table 14, no significant main effects were found for these variables. No significant interaction effects were found.

With respect to motivation Dimension 2, goal orientation, significant main effects were found for both proficiency and gender, but not for age. (Once again, no interaction effects were found.) Bearing in mind that the negative end of this dimension indicates externally referenced goals (both instrumental and integrative) while the positive end refers to internal goals and rewards, the differences shown in Table 13 mean that males in this sample of EFL learners had more externally defined reasons for studying English, while females were more motivated by internal goals. As Table 13 also indicates, there is a steady progression with increasing proficiency toward more tangible reasons for studying English and away from purely internally driven motivational support.

There were significant main effects for age and proficiency on Dimension 3, expectancy. As can be seen in Table 13, scores on this dimension decrease with age and with increasing proficiency and are lower for females than for males. Because of the stringent requirement that $p<.017$, imposed because multiple ANOVAs were been carried out, the effect for gender must be judged statistically non-significant, but in an exploratory analysis this certainly constitutes a trend worthy of comment. A comparison of the means for Dimension 3 in Table 13 indicates that expectation of success declines with age, declines with increasing proficiency, and is somewhat lower for women than for men. Since these findings are counter-intuitive, we will return to the meaning of Dimension 3 in the following section.

DISCUSSION

THE INTERNAL STRUCTURE OF MOTIVATION

The structural components of foreign language motivation found in this study through factor analysis can be compared with those identified in two other recent studies of language learning motivation in foreign language contexts. Dörnyei (1990a) investigated the motivation for learning English of a group of adult learners in Hungary, and Julkunen (1989) investigated the motivational profiles of school children learning English in Finland.

	This study	Dörnyei (1990a)	Julkunen (1989)
Factor 1	Determination	Instrumentality	Communicative orientation
Factor 2	Anxiety	Need for achievement	Intrinsic orientation
Factor 3	Instrumental orientation	Interest in foreign cultures	Attitudes toward teacher/method
Factor 4	Sociability	Values associated w/language	Integrative motivation
Factor 5	Attitudes to foreign culture	Bad learning experiences	Helplessness
Factor 6	Foreign residence	Spend time abroad	Anxiety

Factor 7	Intrinsic motivation	Language learning as challenge	Criteria for success
Factor 8	Beliefs about failure		Latent interest in English
Factor 9	Enjoyment		

In comparing these three studies — looking not only at the labels assigned to each factor by each researcher but also at individual items loading on those factors — a number of similarities and differences can be noted, although it is necessary to be conservative because the questionnaires used were different. In the present study and in Dörnyei's study, but not in Julkunen's study, an instrumental orientation emerged as one factor of motivation. Julkunen's questionnaire did include items indicative of an instrumental orientation toward English, but in the factor analysis these emerged as part of a heterogeneous cluster of items that Julkunen labeled as "communicative orientation." It may be that the instrumental aspects of foreign language learning motivation are more salient for adults who have chosen to study English privately than for children who are taking English as a school subject who are not yet faced with career choices or the need to be concerned with making a living. This study and that of Dörnyei both identified a factor concerned with positive attitudes toward and interest in foreign cultures. In Julkunen's study, similar items were part of what he labeled "integrative orientation," which also included the desire to get to know English people and Americans and willingness to emigrate to England or America, which was a separate factor in the present study ("foreign residence") and in Dörnyei's ("spend time abroad").

In both this study and that of Julkunen, an intrinsic orientation (enjoyment of the study of English for its own sake) was identified. Dörnyei did not assign this label to any factor, but his factor "language learning is a new challenge" can be considered a form of intrinsic motivation (Wong and Csikszentmihalyi, 1991). The present study and that of Julkunen also identified a factor of anxiety, also missing from Dörnyei's results, although his factor labeled "bad learning experiences" (which includes negative evaluations of one's aptitude for language learning) partially overlaps.

Of the three studies, Julkunen's is the only one to identify a clear integrative orientation factor; both this study and that of Dörnyei instead found several factors that can be labeled integrative in at least a weak sense. Julkunen's study is the only one to have identified a motivational factor of attitudes toward teacher and teaching method. In our case, this is because we analyzed preferences for instructional methods and classroom activities separately. Dörnyei did not include items relevant to this construct in his questionnaire.

The present study is the only one that identified a factor of sociability as part of foreign language learning motivation. The sociability factor may be unique to the Egyptian context, but it more likely reflects the fact that other researchers have not often included such items in their questionnaires. In another study of Hungarian learners, Clément, Dörnyei, and Noels (1994) found that in addition to attitude-based and self-confidence-based components of motivation, a third, relatively inde–pendent subprocess of group cohesion emerged in the foreign language classroom.

Each of the three studies provides some evidence of the importance of attributions of success and failure in the structure of motivation for foreign language learning, but in different ways. Julkunen found that items related to internal criteria for success in tasks, answers to teacher's questions, success in exams, and grades formed a clearly differentiated factor in motivation for learning. Dörnyei's factor labeled "bad learning experiences" included items related to attributions of past failures, which he speculated are more important than the perception of failure itself, but his questionnaire contained no items concerning success or attributions about success. In the present study, attributions appear to be different depending on whether one is concerned with failure or success. Statements concerning external causes of failure emerged in our analysis as an independent factor. Statements concerning internal control of success emerged as part of our Factor 1. Although Dörnyei's analysis yielded a need-achievement factor (related to determination) and Julkunen's analysis yielded a factor of helplessness (the opposite of expectations for success), the present study is apparently the first to find a clear relationship between items concerning expectations for success based on the internal factors of ability and effort and determination to succeed, both of which contribute to our Factor 1. This makes good theoretical sense. Expectancy-value models of motivation assume that learners with generally high expectations of success for a specific task (e.g., a language course) will be more involved in the task and persist longer in the face of difficulty than will students with low expectations of success, who will give up more easily (Pintrich, 1988, p. 75).

Multidimensional scaling has not been used before in any studies of foreign language motivation of which we are aware, so no comparisons to other studies are possible. Multidimensional scaling analysis has both strengths and drawbacks. One strength is the ability of MDS to account for more of the observed variation. Our factor analysis of motivation, with nine factors, only accounted for 48% of total variance; multidimensional scaling of the same data produced a three-dimensional solution that accounted for 85% of the variance. The factor analysis of instructional preferences produced a six-factor solution accounting for 50% of the variance; MDS produced a two-dimensional solution accounting for 88% of the variance. The factor analysis of learning strategies accounted for 47% of the variance with five factors, while MDS accounted for 81% with two dimensions. The trade-off was that the dimensions thus identified were harder than factors to identify theoretically, and this was particularly true of the dimensions of motivation, the primary focus of this study.

If we have interpreted these dimensions of motivation correctly (as affect, goal orientation, and expectancy), this amounts to a significant modification of cognitive theories of motivation. We began with a value-expectancy model of motivation that asserts that people engage in activities that are relevant to their goals and at which they expect to succeed. The results of this study indicate that there is a third dimension to motivation: people engage in activities that they enjoy and that do not arouse anxiety. Although most theories of foreign language motivation have given little attention to intrinsic motivation and most investigations of language learning anxiety have treated it as a separate variable from motivation (Horwitz, 1986; Horwitz, Horwitz, and Cope, 1986; MacIntyre and Gardner, 1991a, 1991b), Gottfried (1985) found that intrinsic motivation and anxiety were not independent factors.

Historically, the investigation of motivation in general psychology has moved from purely behavioristic models to cognitive models to models that include both cognition and affect. Our results seem to support this progression. They are also remarkably similar to the results obtained by Ushioda (1992), who investigated Irish learners' motivation for learning French using a qualitative, ethnographic approach and found that from the learners' perspective, the most frequently cited sources of motivation were language-related enjoyment, personal goals, and prior learning experiences. Our results are also similar to Schumann's (1994b) characterization of the factors that determine stimulus appraisals at the neurobiological level: novelty and pleasantness (affect), goal or need significance, and coping mechanisms (expectancy). (Schumann identified a fourth factor, self and social image, that did not emerge as a separate dimension in our analysis.)

Although this suggests a large universal component in motivation for foreign language learning, we also expect that there are culture-specific aspects to the precise definition and content of each dimension. On the dimension of affect, Schmidt and Savage (1992) found little support for Csikszentmihalyi's theory of intrinsic motivation in a study of Thai EFL learners, while this study of Egyptian EFL learners has found support for the theory. We suspect also that the dimension of expectancy may differ in interesting ways in different cultural groups. We have noted the counter-intuitive result that, for this sample of learners, ratings of questionnaire items dealing with expectancy declined with age and with increasing English proficiency. However, in our discussion of the meaning of motivation Dimension 3, we observed that an equally appropriate label for the dimension might be "positive thinking" or even "denial." We think these are probably appropriate labels for this dimension for this population. The original reason for including many of the items concerning expectancy in the questionnaire (e.g., *if I do well in this course it will be because of the teacher; if I don't do well in this class it will be because I don't try hard enough*) was to see if there was a factor of internal versus external attribution, a distinction highlighted in many models of motivation in education. It turned out that there was not, that many informants responded negatively to any mention of failure regardless of the attached attribution. If this denial interpretation is correct, then the negative correlation with age and proficiency represents not low expectations for success but simply more realism. Women, older learners, and more proficient learners do not simply deny all possibility of failure or difficulty. This might have pedagogical implications as well. Many researchers have suggested that one important motivational strategy for foreign language learning is to boost learners' expectations of success (Crookes and Schmidt, 1991; Dörnyei, 1994a; Oxford and Shearin, 1994). This might not be necessary for some learners.

EXTERNAL CONNECTIONS

Motivation, preferences for learning strategies, and preferences for instructional activities and classroom structures are related. Correlations among aspects of motivation identified through factor analysis and factors derived from the analysis of the other parts of our questionnaire turned up numerous significant relationships. Learners high in determination, learners with strong instrumental motivation, and learners motivated by sociability all indicate by their ratings of learning strategies that they are active learners. Determined learners prefer classes in which there is a balance between different skill emphases and a balance between teacher control and student centeredness, together with activities that are challenging. Anxious students, on the other hand, would rather not participate actively in class and don't like activities that force them to, but prefer to be silent. The strongest relationship, supported both by the results based on factor analysis and by those based on multidimensional scaling, is that language learning enjoyment and its opposite, anxiety, are related to attitudes toward traditional class structures and contemporary, communicative ones. Students who score high on the affect dimension of motivation welcome communicative classes; students who score low on this dimension are resistant and tend to reject group and pair work and other aspects of the communicative classroom.

Scores on the dimensions of motivation are also related to age, gender, and language proficiency, with level of English proficiency being most important. More proficient learners of English enjoy language learning more, have more realistic expectations of success, and have a greater appreciation of the benefits of learning English (both instrumental and integrative) than do beginners. This suggests that a pedagogy informed by an appreciation of motivational factors and their interrelationships with the kinds of classes preferred by different types of learners need not reject contemporary communicative approaches, even though some (or even many) learners resist them. From our data it seems likely that this may indeed be a problem with respect to some learners, especially at the lower levels of proficiency, but as proficiency increases, so does enjoyment and with it an appreciation of methods designed to develop communicative proficiency. Our data are not adequate for determining whether it is increased proficiency itself that makes the communicative orientation more attractive or the cumulative effects of exposure to contemporary methods that has occurred along the way.

ACKNOWLEDGMENTS

We acknowledge the support of Richard Seymour, Dean of the College of Language, Linguistics, and Literature at the University of Hawai'i at Mānoa, for the research reported here. We also extend our sincere thanks to Inas Lotfi, Heliopolis Branch Director, Center for Adult and Continuing Education at the American University in Cairo, for allowing us access to a large group of highly motivated learners of EFL and for putting the resources of the branch behind this research project. Sandra Fotos provided helpful comments on an earlier draft of this paper, but, of course, the remaining flaws are our own.

إستبيان رأي

عزيزي الطالب/عزيزتي الطالبة:

يهدف هذا الاستبيان معرفة اهدافكم من دراسة اللغة الانجليزية وذلك حتي نتمكن من تعديل برامجنا واساليبنا التعليمية لكي تلائم احتياجاتكم العملية الفعلية حتي نحقق الغرض المرجو من انشاء هذه البرامج .

الاسم:

السن:

آخر مؤهل دراسي حصلت عليه:

الوظيفة:

عدد دورات اللغة الانجليزية التي اشتركت فيها:

ضع دائرة حول الرقم الذي يعبر عن رأيك في العبارات الآتية:

٦   :   اوافق تماماً

٥   :   اوافق

٤   :   اوافق الي حد ما

٣   :   لا اوافق الي حد ما

٢   :   لا اوافق

١:   لا اوافق علي الاطلاق

١. إنني استمتع جدا بدراسة اللغة الانجليزية.

٦	٥	٤	٣	٢	١

٢. إن دراسة اللغة الانجليزية تعد هواية بالنسبة لي.

٦	٥	٤	٣	٢	١

٣. إن تعلم اللغة الانجليزية بدرجة أكبر يعد تحديا استمتع به.

٦	٥	٤	٣	٢	١

٤. إنني لا استمتع بدراسة اللغة الانجليزية ولكنني أعلم أن تعلم الانجليزية هام جداً بالنسبة لي.

٦	٥	٤	٣	٢	١

٥. أتمنى لو كنت أستطيع تعلم الانجليزية بطريقة أسهل وبدون الذهاب الي الفصل.

٦	٥	٤	٣	٢	١

٦. إن اللغة الانجليزية هامة جداً بالنسبة لي لانها توسع من مداركي.

٦	٥	٤	٣	٢	١

٧. إن السبب الاساسي لاخذي هذا الفصل هو أن والدي/زوجي/زوجتي/رؤسائي يريدونني أن احسن لغتي الانجليزية.

٦	٥	٤	٣	٢	١

٨. أريد أن يكون ادائي في هذا الفصل جيداً لأنه من المهم إبراز قدراتي لعائلتي/ اصدقائي/رؤسائي/آخرين.

٦	٥	٤	٣	٢	١

٩. يجب أن يكون كل المصريين قادرين علي التحدث باللغة الانجليزية.

٦	٥	٤	٣	٢	١

١٠. إن القدرة على التحدث بالإنجليزية سوف ترفع من مستواي الاجتماعي.

٦	٥	٤	٣	٢	١

١١. إنني اتعلم الإنجليزية لأنني اود ان امضي فترة من الزمن في بلد يتكلم اللغة الإنجليزية.

٦	٥	٤	٣	٢	١

١٢. اريد ان اتعلم الإنجليزية لأنها مفيدة عند السفر في بلاد كثيرة.

٦	٥	٤	٣	٢	١

١٣. اريد ان اتعلم الإنجليزية لأنني اود ان اهاجر.

٦	٥	٤	٣	٢	١

١٤. إن احد اسباب تعلمي الإنجليزية هو ان استطيع تكوين اصدقاء جدد في فصل اللغة الإنجليزية.

٦	٥	٤	٣	٢	١

١٥. إنني اتعلم للغة الإنجليزية حتى اصبح علي درجة افضل من التعليم.

٦	٥	٤	٣	٢	١

١٦. تعد القدرة علي قراءة الإنجليزية احد الأمور الهامة في مجالي الحرفي / الاكاديمي.

٦	٥	٤	٣	٢	١

١٧. إن السبب الرئيسي لحاجتي لدراسة اللغة الإنجليزية هو ان انجح في الامتحانات.

     ١   ٢   ٣   ٤   ٥   ٦

١٨. إذا تعلمت اللغة الإنجليزية بطريقة افضل فسوف اكون قادرا علي الحصول علي عمل افضل.

     ١   ٢   ٣   ٤   ٥   ٦

١٩. إن زيادة مهارتي في اللغة الإنجليزية سوف يكون لها فوائد مادية بالنسبة لي.

     ١   ٢   ٣   ٤   ٥   ٦

٢٠. إذا تمكنت من التحدث باللغة الانجليزية فسوف تكون حياتي رائعة.

     ١   ٢   ٣   ٤   ٥   ٦

٢١. إنني اود حقا ان اتعلم الإنجليزية اكثر في هذا الفصل عما تعلمته في الماضي.

     ١   ٢   ٣   ٤   ٥   ٦

٢٢. من المهم بالنسبة لي ان يكون ادائي في الفصل افضل من اداء بقية زملائي.

     ١   ٢   ٣   ٤   ٥   ٦

٢٣. إن علاقتي بالأستاذ في هذا الفصل هامة بالنسبة لي.

     ١   ٢   ٣   ٤   ٥   ٦

٢٤. إن من اهم الأشياء في هذا الفصل هو التفاهم مع الطلاب الآخرين.

     ١   ٢   ٣   ٤   ٥   ٦

٢٥. إن هذا الفصل مهم بالنسبة لي لأنه لو تعلمت الإنجليزية جيدا فسوف اكون قادرا علي مساعدة اطفالي في تعلم الإنجليزية.

     ١   ٢   ٣   ٤   ٥   ٦

٢٦. ان دورة اللغة الإنجليزية هذه سوف تساعدني بالتأكيد في تحسين لغتي الإنجليزية.

     ١   ٢   ٣   ٤   ٥   ٦

٢٧. إذا كان ادائي طيب في هذا لفصل فإن السبب هو انني احاول بجهد.

     ١   ٢   ٣   ٤   ٥   ٦

٢٨. اتوقع ان يكون ادائي طيب في هذا الفصل لأنني جيد في تعلم اللغة الإنجليزية.

     ١   ٢   ٣   ٤   ٥   ٦

٢٩. إذا لم اتعلم جيدا في هذا الفصل فإن السبب هو انني لا احاول بدرجة كافية.

     ١   ٢   ٣   ٤   ٥   ٦

٣٠. إذا لم يكن ادائي طيب في هذا الفصل فإن السبب هو انني ليست لدي قدرة كبيرة لتعلم اللغة الإنجليزية.

     ١   ٢   ٣   ٤   ٥   ٦

٣١. إذا تعلمت الكثير في هذا الفصل فإن الفضل الأول سيرجع الي الأستاذ.

     ١   ٢   ٣   ٤   ٥   ٦

٣٢. إذا كان ادائي طيب في هذا الفصل فإن السبب هو ان هذا فصل سهل.

     ١   ٢   ٣   ٤   ٥   ٦

٣٣. إذا لم اتعلم جيدا في هذا الفصل فإن السبب سوف يرجع الي الأستاذ بالدرجة الأولي.

١   ٢   ٣   ٤   ٥   ٦

٣٤. إذا لم يكن ادائي طيب في هذا الفصل فإن السبب هو ان هذا فصل صعب جدا.

١   ٢   ٣   ٤   ٥   ٦

٣٥. إن الأمريكيين شعب ودود جدا.

١   ٢   ٣   ٤   ٥   ٦

٣٦. يميل الإنجليز الي ان يكونو متكبرين وغير ودودين.

١   ٢   ٣   ٤   ٥   ٦

٣٧. الإنجليز متمسكون بالعادات والتقاليد.

١   ٢   ٣   ٤   ٥   ٦

٣٨. الأمريكيون غير تقليديون.

١   ٢   ٣   ٤   ٥   ٦

٣٩. ان معظم الممثلين والموسيقيين المفضلين عندي بريطانيين او امريكيين.

١   ٢   ٣   ٤   ٥   ٦

٤٠. لقد قدمت الثقافة البريطانية الكثير للعالم.

١   ٢   ٣   ٤   ٥   ٦

٤١. إن الثقافة الأمريكية ليست ذات تأثير مستحب جدا في مصر.

١   ٢   ٣   ٤   ٥   ٦

٤٢. إنني احس بعدم الراحة اذا ما اضطررت الي الحديث في فصل اللغة الإنجليزية.

١   ٢   ٣   ٤   ٥   ٦

٤٣. ان التطوع بالإجابة في فصل اللغة الإنجليزية يسبب لي حرجا.

١   ٢   ٣   ٤   ٥   ٦

٤٤. لا احب ان اتكلم في فصل اللغة الإنجليزية لأنني اخشي ان استاذي سوف يعتقد انني لست طالب جيد.

١   ٢   ٣   ٤   ٥   ٦

٤٥. أخشي ان يسخر الطلاب الأخرين مني عندما اتحدث بالإنجليزية في الفصل.

١   ٢   ٣   ٤   ٥   ٦

٤٦. اعتقد انني استطيع تعلم الإنجليزية جيدا الا انني لا اؤدي جيدا في الأختبارات والامتحانات.

١   ٢   ٣   ٤   ٥   ٦

٤٧. سأسجل لدورة اللغة الإنجليزية القادمة حتي اذا تم رفع المصاريف لأن دراسة اللغة الإنجليزية هامة جدا بالنسبة لي.

١   ٢   ٣   ٤   ٥   ٦

٤٨. إن حضوري في هذا الفصل سوف يكون جيدا.

١   ٢   ٣   ٤   ٥   ٦

٤٩. إنني اخطط للاستمرار في دراسة الإنجليزية لأطول وقت ممكن.

١   ٢   ٣   ٤   ٥   ٦

٥٠. من المحتمل ان آخذ فصل لغة إنجليزية آخر بعد ان انتهي من هذا الفصل.

١   ٢   ٣   ٤   ٥   ٦

٥١. كثيراً ما افكر في كيفية تعلم اللغة الإنجليزية بطريقة افضل.

١   ٢   ٣   ٤   ٥   ٦

٥٢. استطيع ان اقول بأمانة انني ابذل قصاري جهدي في محاولة تعلم اللغة الإنجليزية.

١   ٢   ٣   ٤   ٥   ٦

٥٣. كثيراً ما اجد صعوبة في التركيز أثناء فصل اللغة الإنجليزية.

١   ٢   ٣   ٤   ٥   ٦

٥٤. اود ان يكون الحديث بالإنجليزية فقط خلال حصة اللغة الإنجليزية.

١   ٢   ٣   ٤   ٥   ٦

٥٥. يجب علي الأستاذ ان يشرح اشياء باللغة العربية في بعض الاحيان في حصة اللغة الإنجليزية حتي يساعدنا في التعلم.

١   ٢   ٣   ٤   ٥   ٦

٥٦. من المهم ان يحافظ الأستاذ علي الانضباط داخل حصة اللغة الإنجليزية.

١   ٢   ٣   ٤   ٥   ٦

٥٧. في حصة اللغة الإنجليزية ، يجب ان يؤدي الأستاذ معظم الكلام وان يجاوب الطلبة فقط عندما يطلب منهم ذلك.

١   ٢   ٣   ٤   ٥   ٦

٥٨. يجب علي الطلبة في فصل اللغة الإنجليزية ان يجعلوا الأستاذ يعرف لماذا يدرسون اللغة الإنجليزية وذلك حتي يمكن جعل الدروس مناسبة لاهدافهم.

١   ٢   ٣   ٤   ٥   ٦

٥٩. يجب علي الطلاب ان يسالوا اسئلة عن اي نقطة لا يفهمونها في الحصة.

١   ٢   ٣   ٤   ٥   ٦

٦٠. إنني احب انشطة تعلم الإنجليزية التي يعمل منها الطلاب في ازواج او مجموعات صغيرة.

١   ٢   ٣   ٤   ٥   ٦

٦١. افضل ان اعمل بنفسي وليس مع الآخرين في حصة اللغة الإنجليزية.

١   ٢   ٣   ٤   ٥   ٦

٦٢. إن الأنشطة التي تتم في مجموعات او ازواج من الطلبة في حصة اللغة الإنجليزية تعد مضيعة للوقت.

١   ٢   ٣   ٤   ٥   ٦

٦٣. يجب ان يتأكد الأستاذ ان الجميع يتعلمون الإنجليزية بدرجة متساوية وجيدة في الفصل.

١   ٢   ٣   ٤   ٥   ٦

٦٤. إن فصل اللغة الإنجليزية يكون اكثر افادة عندما يكون التركيز علي قواعد اللغة.

١   ٢   ٣   ٤   ٥   ٦

٦٥. لا يجب ان يكون النطق محل تركيز كبير في فصل اللغة الإنجليزية.

  ١   ٢   ٣   ٤   ٥   ٦

٦٦. يجب التركيز علي القراءة والكتابة في فصل اللغة الإنجليزية.

  ١   ٢   ٣   ٤   ٥   ٦

٦٧. يجب التركيز علي التكلم والاستماع في فصل اللغة الإنجليزية.

  ١   ٢   ٣   ٤   ٥   ٦

٦٨. يجب ان تصمم الأنشطة في هذا الفصل بحيث تساعد الطالب علي تحسين قدرته في التعامل بالإنجليزية

  ١   ٢   ٣   ٤   ٥   ٦

٦٩. تعد انشطة التعامل مضيعة للوقت في هذا الفصل لأنني احتاج فقط الي تعلم ما هو ضروري للنجاح في امتحانات اللغة الإنجليزية

  ١   ٢   ٣   ٤   ٥   ٦

٧٠. في مثل هذا الفصل فإنني افضل انشطة ومواد تتحدي قدراتي حتي استطيع ان اتعلم اكثر.

  ١   ٢   ٣   ٤   ٥   ٦

٧١. في حصة اللغة الإنجليزية ، فأنني افضل انشطة ومواد تثيرفضولي حتي وان كان من الصعب تعلمها.

  ١   ٢   ٣   ٤   ٥   ٦

٧٢. انني افضل فصل اللغة الإنجليزية الذي تتوافر فيه كثير من الأنشطة والتي تسمح لي بالإشتراك بإيجابية.

  ١   ٢   ٣   ٤   ٥   ٦

٧٣. افضل ان اجلس واسمع ولا احب ان اجبر علي الكلام في فصل اللغة الإنجليزي

  ١   ٢   ٣   ٤   ٥   ٦

٧٤. من المهم ان يعطي الأستاذ تغذية رجعية مباشرة داخل الفصل وذلك حتي يعرف الطلبة ما اذا كانت اجابتهم صحيحة ام خطأ.

  ١   ٢   ٣   ٤   ٥   ٦

٧٥. يجب علي الأستاذ الا ينتقد الطلاب الذين يرتكبون اخطاء في الفصل.

  ١   ٢   ٣   ٤   ٥   ٦

٧٦. عندما اتعلم كلمات انجليزية جديدة فانني اتدرب علي قولها بتكرارها مرارا حتي اتمكن من حفظها

  ١   ٢   ٣   ٤   ٥   ٦

٧٧. إنني احاول دائما ان احفظ قواعد النحو.

  ١   ٢   ٣   ٤   ٥   ٦

٧٨. انني اقول واكتب التعبيرات الإنجليزية الجديدة تكرارا وذلك للتدريب عليها.

  ١   ٢   ٣   ٤   ٥   ٦

٧٩. عندما اقرأ شيئا بالإنجليزية فإنني عادة ما اقرأه اكثر من مرة

  ١   ٢   ٣   ٤   ٥   ٦

٨٠. عندما اتعلم كلمة جديدة بالإنجليزية فإنني احاول ان اجد لها علاقة بالكلمات الإنجليزية الأخري التي اعرفها.

١   ٢   ٣   ٤   ٥   ٦

٨١. احاول دائما ان الاحظ اوجه التشابه والاختلاف بين الانجليزية والعربية.

١   ٢   ٣   ٤   ٥   ٦

٨٢. عندما اتعلم قاعدة نحوية جديدة فإنني افكر في علاقتها بالقواعد التي اعلمها بالفعل.

١   ٢   ٣   ٤   ٥   ٦

٨٣. انني اعمل ملخصات لما اتعلمه في فصل اللغة الإنجليزية.

١   ٢   ٣   ٤   ٥   ٦

٨٤. عندما ادرس منهج اللغة الإنجليزية فإنني اختار النقاط الأكثر اهمية واقوم بعمل جداول واشكال توضيحية لنفسي.

١   ٢   ٣   ٤   ٥   ٦

٨٥. عندما لا افهم كلمة في سياق القراءة فإنني احاول ان اخمن معناها من المضمون.

١   ٢   ٣   ٤   ٥   ٦

٨٦. انني اتعلم من اخطائي في استخدام اللغة الإنجليزية وذلك بمحاولة فهم اسباب تلك الأخطاء

١   ٢   ٣   ٤   ٥   ٦

٨٧. انني احاول البحث عن نماذج في اللغة الإنجليزية بدون انتظار الأستاذ حتي يشرح لي القواعد

١   ٢   ٣   ٤   ٥   ٦

٨٨. انني احاول ان اجد معني الكلمة وذلك بتقسيمها الي اجزاء استطيع فهمها.

١   ٢   ٣   ٤   ٥   ٦

٨٩. عند اعداد دروس اللغة الإنجليزية فإنني اقرأ المادة العلمية كلها اولاً حتي احصل علي فكرة عامة عن المادة وكذلك لتحديد النقاط الرئيسية.

١   ٢   ٣   ٤   ٥   ٦

٩٠. عند المذاكرة لامتحان فإنني افكر اولا في اهم النقاط بدلا من مجرد قراءة كل شيء.

١   ٢   ٣   ٤   ٥   ٦

٩١. إنني احاول دائما ان اقيم تقدمي في تعلم الإنجليزية

١   ٢   ٣   ٤   ٥   ٦

٩٢. عند المذاكرة لامتحان فإنني احاول ان احدد المفاهيم التي لا افهمها جيدا.

١   ٢   ٣   ٤   ٥   ٦

٩٣. انني احاول ان اغير طريقتي في المذاكرة وذلك حتي تتلائم مع اسلوب تدريس المعلم

١   ٢   ٣   ٤   ٥   ٦

٩٤. عندما لا اؤدي جيدا في إمتحان (تمرين) فإنني اراجعه وذلك حتي اعرف اخطائي واتاكد من انني افهم كل شيء.

١   ٢   ٣   ٤   ٥   ٦

٩٥. ان لدي مكان معين مخصص للمذاكرة.

١   ٢   ٣   ٤   ٥   ٦

٩٦. انني انظم جدولي لأتاكد من انني اسير بإنتظام مع فصل اللغة الإنجليزية.

١   ٢   ٣   ٤   ٥   ٦

٩٧. غالبا ما اجد انني لا اقضي وقت طويل لمذاكرة اللغة الإنجليزية وذلك بسبب الأنشطة الأخري.

١   ٢   ٣   ٤   ٥   ٦

٩٨. انني ابحث بنشاط عن اناس استطيع ان اتكلم معهم اللغة الإنجليزية.

١   ٢   ٣   ٤   ٥   ٦

٩٩. كلما كان لدي سؤال فإنني اسأل المعلم او احاول ان اجد الإجابة بطريقة اخري.

١   ٢   ٣   ٤   ٥   ٦

١٠٠. إنني اتمكن دئماً علي ايجاد الوقت للتحضير قبل كل حصة لغة انجليزي

١   ٢   ٣   ٤   ٥   ٦

QUESTIONNAIRE (BACK-TRANSLATION FROM ARABIC),
WITH OVERALL MEANS AND STANDARD DEVIATIONS

6	5	4	3	2	1
strongly agree	agree	slightly agree	slightly disagree	disagree	strongly disagree

Part A: Motivation

50 items (α = .802)	Mean	S. D.
Intrinsic motivation (α = .54)		
1 I enjoy learning English very much.	5.580	0.763
2 Learning English is a hobby for me.	4.816	1.407
3 Learning English is a challenge that I enjoy.	5.197	1.111
4 I don't enjoy learning English, but I know that learning English is important for me. (reverse-coded)	4.403	1.700
5 I wish I could learn English in an easier way, without going to class. (reverse-coded)	4.227	1.703
Extrinsic motivation (α = .75)		
6 English is important to me because it will broaden my view.	5.568	0.813
7 The main reason I am taking this class is that my parents/my spouse/my supervisors want me to improve my English.	2.693	1.826
8 I want to do well in this class because it is important to show my ability to my family/friends/supervisors /others.	3.707	1.909
9 Everybody in Egypt should be able to speak English.	4.961	1.249
10 Being able to speak English will add to my social status.	5.051	1.332
11 I am learning English because I want to spend a period of time in an English-speaking country.	4.091	1.627

12	I want to learn English because it is useful when traveling in many countries.	5.336	1.026
13	I want to learn English because I would like to emigrate.	2.552	1.738
14	One reason I learn English is that I can meet new people and make friends in my English class.	3.230	1.554
15	I am learning English to become more educated.	5.428	0.947
16	I need to be able to read textbooks in English.	4.903	1.383
17	The main reason I need to learn English is to pass examinations.	2.044	1.334
18	If I learn English better, I will be able to get a better job.	4.779	1.418
19	Increasing my English proficiency will have financial benefits for me.	4.162	1.573
20	If I can speak English, I will have a marvelous life.	4.726	1.312
Personal goals (α = .60)			
21	I really want to learn more English in this class than I have done in the past.	5.588	0.741
22	It is important to me to do better than the other students in my class.	4.706	1.238
23	My relationship with the teacher in this class is important to me.	5.378	0.906
24	One of the most important things in this class is getting along with the other students.	4.850	1.106
25	This class is important to me because if I learn English well, I will be able to help my children learn English.	5.101	1.250
Expectancy/control components (α = .53)			
26	This English class will definitely help me improve my English.	5.604	0.706
27	If I do well in this course, it will be because I try hard.	5.297	0.825
28	I expect to do well in this class because I am good at learning English.	4.806	0.948
29	If I don't do well in this class, it will be because I don't try hard enough.	4.372	1.392
30	If I don't do well in this class, it will be because I don't have much ability for learning English.	3.145	1.613

31	If I learn a lot in this class, it will be because of the teacher.	5.033	1.092
32	If I do well in this class, it will be because this is an easy class.	3.072	1.425
33	If I don't learn well in this class, it will be mainly because of the teacher.	3.223	1.564
34	If I don't do well in this class, it will be because the class is too difficult.	2.846	1.309
Attitudes (α = .54)			
35	Americans are very friendly people.	4.188	1.314
36	The English are conservative people who cherish customs and traditions.	4.308	1.421
37	Most of my favorite actors and musicians are either British or American.	3.320	1.589
38	British culture has contributed a lot to the world.	4.287	1.189
Anxiety (α = .75)			
39	I feel uncomfortable if I have to speak in my English class.	2.634	1.541
40	It embarrasses me to volunteer answers in my English class.	2.541	1.480
41	I don't like to speak often in English class because I am afraid that my teacher will think I am not a good student.	2.455	1.493
42	I am afraid other students will laugh at me when I speak English.	2.223	1.403
43	I think I can learn English well, but I don't perform well on tests and examinations.	3.320	1.499
44	I often have difficulty concentrating in English class.	3.271	1.411
Motivational strength (α = .63)			
45	If the fees for this class were increased, I would still enroll because studying English is important to me.	4.636	1.528
46	My attendance in this class will be good.	5.317	0.835
47	I plan to continue studying English for as long as possible.	5.444	0.868
48	After I finish this class, I will probably take another English course.	5.301	1.037
49	I often think about how I can learn English better.	5.202	1.034
50	I can honestly say that I really put my best effort into trying to learn English.	5.077	1.050

Part B: Preferences for instructional activities

22 items (α = .589)	Mean	S. D.
1 During English class, I would like to have only English spoken.	4.570	1.527
2 In my English class, the teacher should explain things in Arabic sometimes in order to help us learn.	4.056	1.680
3 It is important for the teacher to maintain discipline in English class.	5.524	0.901
4 In English class, the teacher should do most of the talking and the students should only answer when they are called upon.	3.388	1.714
5 Students in English class should let the teacher know why they are studying English so that the lessons can be made relevant to their goals.	5.031	1.229
6 Student should ask questions whenever they have not understood a point in class.	5.718	0.698
7 I like English learning activities in which students work together in pairs or small groups.	5.010	1.088
8 I prefer to work by myself in English class, not with other students.	2.669	1.513
9 Group activities and pair work in English class are a waste of time.	2.383	1.439
10 The teacher should make sure that everyone in this class learns English equally well.	5.031	1.222
11 English class is most useful when the emphasis is put on grammar.	4.010	1.430
12 Pronunciation should not be an important focus of the English class.	2.201	1.555
13 Reading and writing should be emphasized in English class.	4.826	1.288
14 Listening and speaking should be emphasized in English class.	5.519	0.794
15 Activities in this class should be designed to help the students improve their abilities to communicate in English.	5.595	0.781

16	Communication activities are a waste of time in this class, because I only need to learn what is necessary to pass English examinations.	1.867	1.265
17	In a class like this, I prefer activities and materials that really challenge me so that I can learn more.	4.724	1.317
18	In an English class, I prefer activities and materials that arouse my curiosity even if they are difficult to learn.	4.436	1.370
19	I prefer an English class in which there are lots of activities that allow me to participate actively.	5.105	1.020
20	I prefer to sit and listen, and don't like being forced to speak in English class.	2.704	1.570
21	It is important that the teacher give immediate feedback in class so that students know whether their responses are right or wrong.	5.058	1.093
22	The teacher should not criticize students who make mistakes in class.	4.176	1.809

Part C: Learning strategies

25 items (α = .858)		Mean	S. D.
1	When learning new English words, I say them over and over to memorize them.	5.194	0.975
2	I always try to memorize grammar rules.	4.459	1.356
3	I say or write new expressions in English repeatedly to practice them.	5.002	1.085
4	When I read something in English, I usually read it more than once.	4.922	1.302
5	When I learn a new word in English, I try to relate it to other English words I know.	4.893	1.123
6	I always try to notice the similarities and differences between English and Arabic.	3.994	1.509
7	When I learn a new grammar rule, I think about its relationship to rules I have learned already.	4.525	1.290
8	I make summaries of what I have learned in my English class.	4.327	1.461

9	When I study for my English course, I pick out the most important points and make charts, diagrams, and tables for myself.	4.031	1.424
10	When I do not understand a word in something I am reading, I try to guess its meaning from context.	5.024	1.067
11	I learn from my mistakes in using English by trying to understand the reasons for them.	5.183	0.853
12	I try to look for patterns in English without waiting for the teacher to explain the rules to me.	4.274	1.365
13	I try to find the meaning of a word by dividing it into parts that I understand.	4.251	1.370
14	When preparing my English lessons, I read the material through first to get a general idea of what it is about and what the major points are.	4.870	1.064
15	When studying for a test, first I think about what the most important points are, instead of just reading everything over.	4.242	1.540
16	I always try to evaluate my progress in learning English.	5.189	0.904
17	When studying for a test, I try to determine which concepts I don't understand well.	5.021	0.969
18	I try to change the way I study in order to fit the teacher's teaching style.	4.518	1.352
19	When I don't do well on a test/exercise, I always go back over it to figure it out and make sure I understand everything.	5.233	0.980
20	I have a regular place set aside for studying.	4.501	1.485
21	I arrange my schedule to make sure that I keep up with my English class.	4.649	1.230
22	I often find that I don't spend much time studying English because of other activities.	4.169	1.343
23	I actively look for people with whom I can speak English.	4.885	1.134
24	Whenever I have a question, I ask my teacher about it or try to find the answer in another way.	5.108	0.894
25	I always arrange time to prepare before every English class.	4.315	1.353

Zoltán Dörnyei
Eötvös University, Budapest

CHAPTER 3
MOVING LANGUAGE LEARNING MOTIVATION TO A LARGER PLATFORM FOR THEORY AND PRACTICE

ABSTRACT

This chapter explains a significant movement in research on second language learning motivation. A number of researchers have extended the boundaries of such motivation well beyond the parameters set by social psychological theory. In this chapter, the author shares his views on needed expansions of the theory and presents an empirical study supporting a broadened theory. Some important individual difference variables at the language level, the learner level, and the learning situation level are examined in this chapter. The chapter ends with a set of specific recommendations for future research.

INTRODUCTION

This chapter discusses a major shift in research on second language learning motivation that has been taking place over the last five years. During this time several researchers (e.g., Brown, 1990, 1994; Clément, Dörnyei and Noels, 1994; Crookes and Schmidt, 1991; Dörnyei, 1994a, 1994b; Oxford and Shearin, 1994; Skehan, 1991) have attempted to reopen the agenda of motivation research by suggesting modifications to Robert Gardner's and his associates' social psychological construct of language learning motivation (e.g., Gardner, 1985b; Gardner and Clément, 1990; Gardner and MacIntyre, 1993) and introducing new concepts rooted in other areas of psychology. These attempts might have been understood by some as attacks on Gardner's motivation theory, but I do not think that this was really the case. The explicit goal of recent research has been to broaden the scope of language learning motivation and to increase the educational potential of the theory by focusing more on motivation as reflected in students' classroom learning behaviors. However, none of the authors have rejected Gardner's construct in their attempts to do this.

In Central Europe, ethnolinguistic attitudes have always played a particularly salient role (we should only think of the numerous ethnic conflicts currently taking place in the region). Coming from Hungary, I have never questioned the relevance of a social psychological approach to understanding language learning motives. Most nations in the world are multicultural, and the majority of people in the world speak

Dörnyei, Zoltán (1996). Moving language learning motivation to a larger platform for theory and practice. In Rebecca Oxford (Ed.), *Language Learning Motivation: Pathways to the New Century*. (Technical Report #11) (pp. 71–80). Honolulu: University of Hawai'i, Second Language Teaching & Curriculum Center.

at least one second language. These facts underscore the importance of the social dimension of language learning motivation. What I believe, however, is that this social dimension is not the only major constituent of language learning motivation: indeed, from an educational perspective, it may not even be the most important one. Motivation to learn a second language is a complex and eclectic psychological construct that involves several non-social factors as well. This is not surprising if we consider the following:

1. Motivation theories in general want to explain the fundamental question of why humans behave as they do, and therefore we cannot assume any simple and straightforward answer. In fact, every different psychological perspective of human behavior will come up with a different theory of motivation, and thus in general psychology it is not the lack but rather the abundance of motivation theories that confuses the scene.

2. Motivation to learn a second language presents a unique situation even within motivational psychology due to the multifaceted nature and role of language. Language is at the same time: (1) a communication coding system that can be taught as a school subject; (2) an integral part of the individual's identity involved in almost all mental activities (just think of sentences like "This doesn't sound like me"); and also (3) the most important channel of social organization embedded in the culture of the community where it is used. Thus, if language serves all these purposes, then language learning motivation will also contain — besides the social dimension — an educational and a personal dimension. The main direction of recent research on motivation can be characterized by shifting the focus from the social dimension to these latter dimensions.

BROADENING THE RESEARCH PARADIGM

In the mid–1980s I conducted research among Hungarian learners of English to investigate the difference between motivation in a foreign language learning and a second language acquisition environment (Dörnyei, 1990a). This research was determined by a social psychological approach rooted in the Canadian tradition, and even though the emerging construct of language learning motivation showed some deviations from the construct developed in Canada, these could be explained by contextual differences while still maintaining a social psychological perspective. Interestingly, it was the lack of some expected results in the follow-up of this research (Dörnyei, 1990b) that proved to be more significant than the detected differences in the long run.

Table 1: Correlations between motivational components and four criterion measures: Course Achievement, Course Attendance, Further Enrollment, and Extracurricular Language Use (Dörnyei, 1990b, pp. 9–10)

	Course Achievement	Course Attendance	Further Enrollment	Extracurricular Language Use
INSTRUMENTAL MOTIVATIONAL SUBSYSTEM				
Instrumental language use	–.04	–.04	.06	–.04
Instrumentality	–.06	.06	.06	.15
Desire to integrate into a new community				
Desire to spend some time abroad	–.23*	.00	–.19*	.02
INTEGRATIVE MOTIVATIONAL SUBSYSTEM				
Interest in foreign languages, cultures, and people				
Passive sociocultural language use	.07	.05	.04	.18*
Interest in foreign languages and cultures	.15	–.05	–.05	.42***
Desire to keep up-to-date and to avoid provincialism				
Reading for nonprofessional purposes	.02	–.19*	.05	.08
Desire for knowledge and values associated with English	–.04	–.14	.10	–.05
Desire for challenge				
Active sociocultural language use	–.21*	–.17*	–.03	.24**
Language learning is a new challenge	–.07	–.10	–.07	.00
NEED FOR ACHIEVEMENT				
Need for achievement	.18*	.06	.18*	.16
ATTRIBUTIONS ABOUT PAST FAILURES				
Bad learning experiences	–.11	.01	–.05	.03

* $p<.05$ ** $p<.01$ ***$p<.001$

In this follow-up study I correlated the obtained motivational components with four classroom learning-specific criterion measures: course achievement, further enrollment in the language course, course attendance, and extracurricular language use. These criterion measures are undoubtedly key factors in the language learning process and still, as can be seen in Table 1, hardly any significant correlations emerged between them and the motivational factors found. Only extracurricular language use (i.e., seeking contact with foreigners) showed a considerable positive relationship with some integrative motives. The remaining classroom-related measures simply did not appear to be related to the motives I found.

What happened? Why did the motivational components identified in my research not affect learning behaviors observed with the same subjects? The answer I came up with was that these behaviors were closely connected to the classroom level of the learning process and must have been energized by motivational factors — particularly those related to the actual classroom milieu — that were simply not included in the original research paradigm and therefore could not show up in my factor analytical study. However, this was only an assumption, requiring further research to confirm it.

To shed light on this puzzle, Richard Clément, Kim Noels and I designed and carried out a second project in Hungary, in which we surveyed Hungarian secondary school learners of English (ages 17–18), using a significantly extended research paradigm, including scales focusing on some learner traits as well as the learners' perception of the classroom environment and the dynamics of the learner group (Clément, Dörnyei, and Noels, 1994). The study was carefully administered in order to obtain reliable data about sensitive issues such as the evaluation of the language teacher, and was accompanied by a teacher questionnaire in which we gathered information about the subjects to serve as criterion measures. The results produced evidence that motivation to learn a foreign language in a classroom environment entails more than a social and pragmatic aspect. As Figure 1 shows, we identified three distinct dimensions:

Figure 1. Schematic representation of the tripartite construct of L2 motivation (Clément, Dörnyei, and Noels, 1994, p. 441)

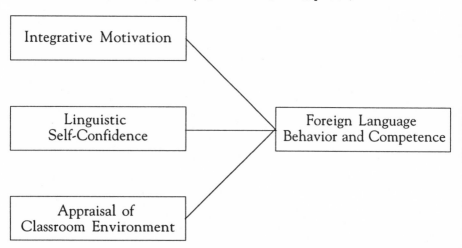

1. Integrative motivation, which is the central component of the social dimension of language learning motivation. Learners who have more favorable attitudes toward the second language, the second language speakers, the values the second language conveys, and the knowledge of

the second language, are likely to be more successful language learners than others with less favorable attitudes.

2. Linguistic self-confidence, including language anxiety, which is a central component in the personal dimension of motivation. Learners who are less anxious, have better previous experiences with using the second language, who evaluate their own proficiency more highly, and who consider the learning tasks less difficult — in short, who are more self-confident about their second language learning and use — are more motivated to learn the second language than those whose motivation is hindered by a lack of self-confidence.

It should be noted that the emergence of self-confidence as a distinct factor was not unexpected. Clément and his colleagues (Clément, 1980; Clément and Kruidenier, 1985; Labrie and Clément, 1986) have produced sufficient evidence that self-confidence is a powerful motivational process in multi-ethnic, multilingual settings, and our study showed that self-confidence is also a major motivational subsystem in foreign language learning situations (i.e., where there is no direct contact with members of the L2 community).

3. Appraisal of the classroom environment. The emergence of this dimension of language learning motivation was the most novel result of the study, and therefore a more detailed description follows.

It has been pointed out several times in the second language literature that the difficulty of understanding the exact nature of classroom events lies to a large extent in the complexity of the classroom. In our attempt to find a scientific construct that would cover a large number of classroom phenomena, we applied a group dynamics-based approach. Three aspects of the students' perception of the classroom assessed were:

*   group cohesion (i.e., how "together" the group is);
*   evaluation of the English teacher in terms of competence, rapport, motivation (i.e., enthusiasm and commitment), and teaching style/personality; and
*   evaluation of the English course in terms of attractiveness, relevance, and difficulty.

Apart from course difficulty, which loaded on self-confidence, all the other classroom-related factors appeared to form a cluster centered around the appraisal of the classroom environment, and this cluster correlated significantly with foreign language behaviors and competence. Thus, our study confirmed language teachers' intuitive knowledge that what goes on in the classroom will considerably affect the learners' affective predisposition.

An interesting aspect of the results was the lack of a major motivational component, namely that of instrumental motivation. Instrumental orientation in our study clustered together with knowledge orientation, and this joint factor loaded onto the integrative motive. Why did this happen? I believe that instrumental motivation is a central component of motivation where it is relevant, that is, where relatively short-term pragmatic, utilitarian benefits are actually available for the learners. If by such benefits we mean job- or salary-related motives, instrumental motivation is actually very often not too relevant to school kids. For the secondary school students in our study, pragmatic rewards appeared quite remote, and the wish to prepare for a bright career was related to getting higher qualifications, and thus to obtaining knowledge.

Our research was not alone in pointing out the significance of situation-specific motives. Researchers such as Kiösti Julkunen (1989, 1991), Douglas Brown (1990, 1994), Peter Skehan (1991), Graham Crookes and Richard Schmidt (1991), and Rebecca Oxford and Jill Shearin (1994), in various parts of the world, have come to very similar conclusions, suggesting a wide range of new concepts to be exploited. The papers in this volume offer a good summary of the ideas that have been put forward to elaborate on the construct of motivation. In the following, I would like to present a framework that might be used to bring together many different lines of research.

A FRAMEWORK FOR LANGUAGE LEARNING MOTIVATION

The framework presented in Figure 2 is based on the Clément et al. (1994) study mentioned earlier but has been broadened in scope. Three levels of motivation are distinguished: the language level, the learner level, and the learning situation level. The three levels coincide with the three basic constituents of the second language learning process (the target language, the language learner, and the language learning environment), and also reflect the three different aspects of language mentioned earlier (the social dimension, the personal dimension, and the educational subject matter dimension). For a detailed description of the constituents of these motivational levels the reader is referred to Dörnyei (1994a); here I will provide only a brief characterization of them.

Figure 2. Components of foreign language learning motivation
(Dörnyei, 1994a, p. 280)

LANGUAGE LEVEL   Integrative Motivational Subsystem
Instrumental Motivational Subsystem

LEARNER LEVEL   Need for Achievement
Self-Confidence
- Language Use Anxiety
- Perceived L2 Competence
- Causal Attributions
- Self-Efficacy

LEARNING SITUATION LEVEL

Course-Specific Motivational Components	Interest Relevance Expectancy Satisfaction

Teacher-Specific Motivational Components	Affiliative Drive
	Authority Type
	Direct Socialization of Motivation
	   • Modeling
	   • Task Presentation
	   • Feedback

Group-Specific Motivational Components	Goal-orientedness Norm and Reward System Group Cohesion Classroom Goal Structure

The language level of motivation concerns ethnolinguistic, cultural-affective, intellectual, and pragmatic values and attitudes attached to the target language; these values and attitudes are, to a large extent, determined by the social milieu in which the learning takes place. A comprehensive way of describing the motivational processes at this level is by using the traditional concepts of integrative and instrumental motivation.

The learner level concerns various fairly stable personality traits that the learner has developed in the past. Some of these are language-specific (e.g., many components of linguistic self-confidence), some others are related to learning and achieving in general (e.g., need for achievement).

The learning situation level is associated with situation-specific motives rooted in various aspects of language learning in a classroom setting. Within this level, three main types of motivational sources can be separated:

1. Course-specific motivational components, which are related to the syllabus, the teaching materials, the teaching method, and the learning tasks.

2. Teacher-specific motivational components, which are related to the teacher's behavior, personality, and teaching style.

3. Group-specific motivational components, which are related to the dynamics of the learner group.

The rationale for separating the three motivational levels is that they seem to have a vital effect on the overall motivation independently of each other; that is, by changing the parameters at one level and keeping the other two dimensions constant, the overall motivation might completely change. For example, the same learner in the same learning situation might show a strikingly different degree of motivation depending on what the target language is. Similarly, when the target language is the same, the same learner's motivation can show vast differences as the function of the learning situation, that is, the appraisal of the language classroom (just think of the potential effect of a bad or a good teacher). In other words, each of the three levels of motivation exert their influence independently of the others and have enough power to nullify the effects of the motives associated with the other two levels.

DIRECTIONS FOR FUTURE RESEARCH

In this last section I will list a number of directions for future research on motivation which I consider potentially very fruitful.

1. Specifying the new theories in sufficient detail to make them testable. In order to achieve the required precision, all the constituent components of motivation must be explicitly defined and assumptions must be made about their interrelationships. Because recent motivational innovations have borrowed from a wide range of systems within various branches of psychology, only by conceptualizing constructs in concrete terms can we hope to integrate the various factors in one coherent framework.

2. Deciding how new motivational concepts are related to established motivational factors such as the integrative motive or linguistic self-confidence, and determining in what way the new constructs can offer more than the old paradigms.

3. Focusing more on how to motivate language learners and test the efficiency of motivating strategies suggested recently in the literature. Such research could, eventually, catalogue the motivational background of various language teaching methodological approaches, and could help us understand the affective foundation of the teaching process.

4. Examining motivation as a function of time. So far motivation research has primarily focused on describing motivation at a given point in time (i.e., synchronically), and hardly any studies have investigated how motivation changes with time, or what patterns of motivational sequences can energize long-lasting learning processes.

5. Exploring the relationships between motivation and cognitive mental operations. Crookes and Schmidt highlighted the micro-level of motivational effects on second language acquisition, pointing out the relationship between attention and motivation. In general psychology there have been a few studies examining the motivational correlates of "deep" and "superficial" learning, and this line of research would be particularly relevant to language studies.

---

6. Finally, I would like to describe the line of research I am currently most interested in, the analysis of the motivation-behavior-outcome chain by breaking up these components into subunits.

Figure 3 presents a schematic representation of the major components of the chain: Motivation leads to learning behavior, which in turn results in cognitive learning processes, which lead to learning outcomes, including language proficiency. Motivational studies in the past have either explicitly or implicitly relied on this conceptualization when they correlated motivation with language proficiency measures.

Figure 3. The motivation-learning outcome chain

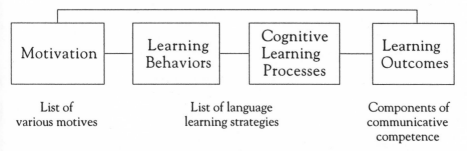

By now it has become obvious that none of the components in Figure 4 are homogeneous. Motivation can be subdivided into a range of motives, as was done in Figure 2. Language learning is not a unified process either but involves a number of diverse behaviors and mental operations, ranging from paying attention in the language class and actively participating in role-play tasks, to grasping every opportunity to talk to native speakers of the target language or doing extensive reading to extend one's vocabulary. The behaviors and mental operations associated with language learning have recently been the focus of attention in learning strategy research, and, indeed, a particularly fruitful direction of research could involve connecting motivation to learning strategies, perceiving the latter as examples of motivated learning behaviors. Learning outcomes can be divided into linguistic and nonlinguistic outcomes, and the former can be further broken down into the various components of communicative competence.

Thus, instead of a straightforward relationship between a limited number of components, a more elaborate representation of the motivation-outcome chain would involve a minimum of three or four lists of variables. The relationship between these variables would be very complex: Some motives will energize certain behaviors but not others. Some learning behaviors will promote certain cognitive processes while leaving other processes unaffected. Some learning behaviors and processes will develop only certain aspects of one's communicative competence. By examining these patterns of causal relationships, motivation research could be connected to other research areas such as research on learning strategies, communicative competence, or language teaching methods, and thus motivation could be more organically integrated into mainstream applied linguistics.

CONCLUSION

In summary, we can conclude that motivation research has gained new momentum in the last few years and has reached an interesting level of development. Let me highlight two aspects of this: (1) Motivation constructs suggested in the literature are about to reach a degree of elaboration that makes them sufficiently adaptable to make motivation assessment a potentially useful tool for both practitioners and researchers working in diverse learning environments pursuing diverse goals. (2) The emerging motivation theories allow for a more organic integration of motivation research into applied linguistic research by combining motivation theory with research topics such as learning strategies, communicative competence, and teaching methodology. In the long run this could bring together two research orientations that have been rather independent in the past: linguistics-based and psychology-based approaches to the study of second language acquisition.

Madeline Ehrman
Foreign Service Institute

CHAPTER 4

AN EXPLORATION OF ADULT LANGUAGE LEARNER MOTIVATION, SELF-EFFICACY, AND ANXIETY

ABSTRACT

This chapter discusses a large empirical study of foreign language learners at the US Foreign Service Institute. Students were typically well-educated and carefully selected for language study. They and their teachers provided perceptions of motivation. Teachers' perceptions of students' extrinsic motivation and students' own intrinsic motivation correlated significantly with end-of-training language performance. Some anomalous results suggest that language learning motivation perhaps should be considered in highly situational and person-related ways.

INTRODUCTION

This paper reports on findings from an ongoing investigation of individual difference variables among adult foreign language learners at the Foreign Service Institute. The focus of this paper is affective variables. Findings from this investigation for other variables have been reported elsewhere: general correlational relationships (Ehrman and Oxford, 1995), ego boundaries (Ehrman, 1993), personality type (Ehrman, 1994a), learning strategies (Oxford and Ehrman, 1995), tested language aptitude (Ehrman, in press), and a study of extremely strong and weak learners (Ehrman, 1994a).

Affective factors have been addressed in all the above-cited papers, but not as the central focus. The present study addresses initial findings from two instruments designed for use in the FSI study; the Affective Survey (Ehrman and Oxford, 1991) and the Language Learning Motivation and Strategies Questionnaire (Christensen and Ehrman, 1993). The two survey instruments are described in the Appendix. Because both instruments are still in the process of validation, and because this study is an early use of both, the present paper should be considered exploratory, not definitive. Further analysis is needed and will be reported on when done.

REVIEW OF LITERATURE

Important aspects of active current research into language learning motivation and anxiety described elsewhere in this volume provide part of the context of the

Ehrman, Madeline (1996). An exploration of adult language learner motivation, self-efficacy, and anxiety. In Rebecca Oxford (Ed.), *Language Learning Motivation: Pathways to the New Century*. (Technical Report #11) (pp. 81–103). Honolulu: University of Hawai'i, Second Language Teaching & Curriculum Center.

investigation described in this paper. The present work is also done in a historical context of investigations undertaken by applied linguists at least since the 1970s and by social, clinical, and experimental psychologists throughout this century. Pioneering work in applied linguistics into the influences of affective factors was done by Guiora (e.g., 1984), Schumann (1978), Gardner and his colleagues (e.g., Gardner, 1985b), and Horwitz and her colleagues (Horwitz, 1985; Horwitz et al., 1986). All of these scholars have had a substantial influence on the field of applied linguistics. Recent work in the area of motivation (Crookes and Schmidt, 1991; Dörnyei, 1994a; Oxford and Shearin, 1994; Gardner and Tremblay, 1994a, 1994b) and other works in this volume rely in part on these theories but also bring into the field of language learning motivation both classic and current work from mainstream branches of psychology.

Rather than duplicate the thorough reviews of literature provided elsewhere in this volume (see especially Chapters 2 and 6), I refer the reader to those papers and to Ehrman and Oxford (1995) and Oxford and Ehrman (1993). For an overview of some clinical perspectives on learning, the reader can refer to my paper on ego boundaries (Ehrman, 1993), in which there is a thorough review of literature related to the effects of ego permeability and identity formation factors on learning and learning motivation.

Here I will provide a brief overview of some research from the educational psychology literature. The three areas of affective variables addressed in this paper are motivation per se, self-efficacy, and anxiety. These classifications also appear often in educational psychology research. The brief review of literature below is therefore presented according to these three categories.

MOTIVATION

New attempts to bring together varying characteristics of motivational differences are being done in the context of cognitive activities and instructional design implications (e.g., Kanfer, 1990). Adaptive instruction programs make use of the constructs of extrinsic and intrinsic motivation and attempt to promote intrinsic motivation among students in a variety of subjects (e.g., Lepper et al., 1992). Another effort to influence motivation suggests that motivational interventions can interfere with effective learning early in skill acquisition, though they may be more effective at later stages of learning (Kanfer and Ackerman, 1989). Studies are finding that effects of motivation in the form of interest in a subject are similar in intensity to effects of ability, and there are effects on quality of cognitive processing related to interest (e.g., Renninger et al., 1992).

SELF-EFFICACY

Multiple studies have shown the predictive effects of self-efficacy on academic achievement (see Schunk, 1991). Self-efficacy can vary according to subject matter or learning context. It can be modified and also applies to teacher behavior as well as student behavior (Gallagher, 1994). Gallagher also points out that level of self-esteem does, of course, have a reciprocal relationship with success in one's endeavors, as well as being a somewhat stable trait. Students who perceive their own ability as low and who believe that ability is fixed also limit their own achievement (Dweck and Leggett, 1988).

ANXIETY

Snow and Swanson (1992, p. 600) state, "Anxiety is the most studied motivational aptitude. Its interaction with instructional treatment seems similar to that of [general intelligence]; high teacher structure is best for more anxious students; low teacher structure is best for less anxious students." Anxiety also interacts with ability (Snow, 1989). Indeed, at least one study indicates that anxiety joins achievement motivation, intrinsic motivation, casual attribution, and expectancy-value instrumentality in correlating with ratings of academic motivation by teachers (Lens and DeCruyenaere, 1991). Many of these findings are corroborated by the results described below.

METHODS

SETTING

The Foreign Service Institute is the training branch of the US Department of State. It offers long-term intensive training in 63 languages of interest to the foreign affairs community. Students are foreign affairs agency employees with job-related needs for language, and adult members of their families. The maximum length of training is 24 weeks in Western European languages, 88 weeks in Arabic, Chinese, Japanese, and Korean, and 44 weeks in almost all others. In most language sections, training relies on communicative methodology 60–80% of the time. End-of-training ratings, based on interviews, are given in speaking (includes interactive comprehension) and reading.

SAMPLE

The total sample consisted of 1,109 people, 55% male and 45% female. (Number of participants for each of the instruments used are lower and represent subsamples.) Most of the group (71%) were from the Department of State, while 10% were from the Defense Department, 8% were from the US Information Agency, 7% were from the Agency for International Development, and the rest (4%) were from other government agencies such as the Department of Agriculture, the Department of Commerce, and the Drug Enforcement Agency. Of the total sample, 83% were employees, and 17% were spouses or college-age children.

With a mean age of 39 (SD = 9), the sample was older than most found in research on language learning. The participants were highly educated. Forty percent had master's degrees, while another 35% had bachelor's degrees. Approximately 15%

had either a high school diploma or a two-year associate degree. Approximately 9% held law degrees or doctorates. Two percent were unaccounted for educationally.

For 99% of the sample, English was the native language. Most of the students were experienced language learners. Twenty-five percent of the students had studied three or more foreign languages previous to beginning this round of training; 23% had studied two foreign languages; 23% had studied one foreign language; and only 10% claimed no foreign language study. Data on language study were unavailable for 19% of the sample.

Sample members were receiving training in 34 languages. Slightly less than one third each were learning Spanish (29.6%) and French (28.5%). In order of numbers of students, the other 32 languages were Italian, Portuguese, Chinese, Arabic, Russian, Thai, Turkish, Hebrew, German, Dutch, Urdu, Indonesian, Burmese, Polish, Romanian, Serbo-Croatian, Greek, Japanese, Korean, Czech, Danish, Hindi, Bengali, Afrikaans, Finnish, Norwegian, Bulgarian, Cantonese, Lao, Swahili, Swedish, and Tagalog.

DATA COLLECTION

Data collection was undertaken by questionnaire. Students were asked to complete a biographical data form and between one and seven instruments examining aptitude, learning strategies, and learning styles, based on a random-sampling procedure. No measures were repeated. All the instruments are described in the Appendix.

The instruments of focus in this paper are the Affective Survey (AFF) and the Language Learning Motivation and Strategies Questionnaire (MSQ), both developed for this study. The Affective Survey was administered midway through the training for part of the sample; the MSQ was administered at the beginning of training for a largely different subsample. Main categories for the Affective Survey are shown in Table 1; Table 2 shows all the affective items for the Motivation and Strategies Questionnaire and a sample of the strategy items. Table 3 lists the other instruments used in the study.

Table 1: The Affective Survey (AFF): Outline of categories (N = 211)

Scale Name in Test	Full Scale Name
MOTIVATION	
Intrinsic*	Self-reported Intrinsic Motivation
Extrinsic*	Self-reported Extrinsic Motivation
Outside Class	Desire to Use Language Outside Class
Effort	Self-reported Application of Effort
SELF-EFFICACY	
Beliefs about Self	Beliefs about Self as a Language Learner*
ANXIETY	
Public Performance**	Anxiety about Public Performance (Speaking in the Classroom)*
Native Speakers	Anxiety about Use with Native Speakers
Correction	Anxiety about Making Errors and Being Corrected*
Comprehension	Anxiety about Comprehension of Over-the-Head Material (listening and reading)
Self-Esteem	Anxiety about Maintaining Self-Esteem*
Competition	Anxiety about Competition
Tests	Anxiety about Tests
Outcomes	Anxiety about Outcomes (grades, final ratings)
Discomfort	General Discomfort with Language Learning
Negative	Negatively Phrased Items (a subset extracted from the above items)*

*   Main variables addressed in this paper
** Unlike the other anxiety scales, "Public Performance" correlates positively with learning success and appears to be a measure of either facilitating anxiety or self-efficacy (Ehrman and Oxford, 1995).

Table 2: The Language Learning Motivation and Strategies Questionnaire (MSQ) (N = 254)

M1: How do you rate your own *ability to learn foreign languages relative to other Americans* in general? (poor, below average, average, above average, superior).*

M2: How do you rate your own *ability to learn foreign languages relative to other FSI students* you have known? (Omit if this is your first FSI experience.) (rated on same scale as MI)*

M3: *How well do you think you will do* in this language course? (rated on same scale as M1)*

M4: How *motivated* are you to learn the language you are going to study now? (not at all, not very much, sufficiently, very much, highly/very much)*

M5: *Considering your own career goals, how much are you looking forward* to studying this language? (same as M4)*

M6: How much do you *want to go to the country* you have been assigned to? (same as M4)*

M7: (interest in non-Western language)

M8: Check off applicable items from list of *common motivators*: M8 items are grouped into two composite variables, extrinsic and intrinsic.

Extrinsic: getting off language probation, incentive payment, need it to do job, want to be best in class, hope for an award;

Intrinsic: language learning is fun, like the country I'm going to, a real challenge, enjoy talking with the people who speak the language, love learning something new, other.*

M9: I would say my *anxiety* about learning this language is: (none at all, not very much, a fair amount, a lot, really nervous about it).*

M10: My *anxiety about speaking in class* (answering questions, giving reports, asking questions, etc.) is about this level: (none at all, not very much, a fair amount, a lot, really nervous about it).*

* Asterisk indicates items of focus for this paper. Words and phrases are shown in *italics* for purposes of clarity in the paper; this is not done in the survey.

There are 43 items rated on a Likert Scale of A: Waste of time, B: Not very helpful, C: Neither/nor, D: Helpful, E: Nearly indispensable.

For example:

1. The instructor systematically follows a textbook or syllabus.

Table 3: Other instruments[1]

Overall Relative to Other FSI Students (O)

Relative Observed Language Learning Aptitude (O)

Achievement Percentage Attributable to Aptitude

Achievement Percentage Attributable to Effort

Level of Effort in Class (O)

Level of Effort Outside Class (O)

Intrinsic Motivation

Extrinsic Motivation

Level of Observed Anxiety in Learning

Hartmann Boundary Questionnaire (HBQ) N = 248

Boundaries between States of Wakefulness

Unusual Experiences (e.g., ESP)

Boundaries between Thinking and Feeling States

Impressions of Childhood, Adulthood

Interpersonal Distance

Physical and Emotional Sensitivity

Dislike for Neatness and Order

Dislike for Clear (Visual) Lines

Opinions about Children, Adolescents, Adults

Opinions about Lines of Authority

Opinions about Ethnic Divisions

Opinions about Abstract Concepts

Total Score

Modern Language Aptitude Test (MLAT) N = 122, Index Score, N = 131

Part I: Number Learning

Part II: Phonetic Script

Part III: Spelling Clues

Part IV: Words in Sentences

Part V: Paired Associates

Total Score

Index Score

continued...

---

[1] All variables are considered continuous (interval) unless otherwise marked by (O) for ordinal or (C) for categorical.

Table 3: Other instruments (cont.)

Myers-Briggs Type Indicator (MBTI) N = 250

Extroversion/Introversion (E/I)   Thinking/Feeling (T/F)

Sensing/Intuition (S/N)   Judging/Perceiving (J/P)

(MBTI Type Differentiation Indicator (TDI) Subscales) N = 250

(Extroversion-Introversion Subscales)   *(Sensing-Intuition Subscales)*

S1 Gregarious-Intimate   S8 Concrete-Abstract

S2 Enthusiastic-Quiet   S9 Realistic-Imaginative

S3 Initiator-Receptor   S10 Pragmatic-Intellectual

S4 Expressive-Contained   S11 Experiential-Theoretical

S5 Auditory-Visual   S12 Traditional-Original

(Thinking-Feeling Subscales)   *(Judging-Perceiving Subscales)*

S14 Critical-Accepting   S21 Stress Avoider-Polyactive

S15 Tough-Tender   S22 Systematic-Casual

S17 Questioning-Accommodating   S23 Scheduled-Spontaneous

S19 Logical-Affective   S24 Planful-Open-ended

S20 Reasonable-Compassionate   S25 Methodical-Emergent

(TDI Comfort-Discomfort Subscales)

S6 Intrepid-Inhibited (also E/I)

S7 Leader-Follower (also E/I)

S13 Guarded-Optimistic (also T/F)

S16 Defiant-Compliant (also T/F)

S18 Carefree-Worried (also T/F)

S26 Decisive-Ambivalent (also J/P)

S27 Proactive-Distractible (also J/P)

Strain (Comfort/Discomfort Composite)

End-of-Training Speaking Proficiency Rating (includes Interactive Comprehension) (EOTS)

End-of-Training Reading Proficiency Rating (EOTR)

DATA ANALYSIS

These tests used Pearson's on SPSS for Windows version 6.1 (Norusis, 1994). All tests of correlational significance were two-tailed.

I have included very low correlations (minimum .11) because (1) this is a preliminary and exploratory study, and (2) the intent is to examine the structure of the constructs, not necessarily to find predictive power. Though low, these correlations appear to pattern consistently across the data to provide an increasingly clear picture of the makeup of FSI learners (and perhaps others). Furthermore, although .11 is very low, I report findings at this level so that later research can further test them with other populations. The acceptable significance level is set at the .05 level for this study. (Significance of .05 is indicated by *, .01 by **, and .001 by ***.) Although the .05 level can result in a high absolute number of errors in view of the large number of variables, again it is used because this is an exploratory study suggesting possible trends for further analysis. In fact, other analyses have tended to bear out trends suggested by the correlations for AFF (this is the first study using MSQ) and even strengthened the inferences made on the basis of some of the lower correlations in this study (see Ehrman, 1993, 1994a, 1994b; Ehrman and Oxford, 1995).

RESULTS

Data from the AFF and the MSQ work well within the three main affective categories described above in the literature review: *motivation* (desire to learn), *self-efficacy* (expectation of ability to cope), and *anxiety* (arousal, usually based in fear). Although there is some overlap among these categories and, as suggested by the Lens and DeCruyenaere (1991) study cited above, they covary relative to teacher motivation ratings, patterns of correlation suggest that they are not the same.

MOTIVATION

Students generally perceive themselves as *intrinsically* motivated in their self-report on the AFF and the MSQ; however, their teachers perceive them as more *extrinsically* motivated, and this is the way I experience them in my interviews with them. A pattern of correlation of MSQ M4, M5, M6 (see Table 2 for these items) with MBTI thinking suggests a considerable instrumental and extrinsic component to out students' motivation as well (thinking tends to be task-focused, in contrast to feeling-focused, which is more person- and value-oriented).[2]

Intrinsic motivation

MSQ intrinsic correlates with other motivation questions (MSQ M4 .23*, M5 .28*, M6 .16*) self-efficacy (M1 .17**, and AFF beliefs about self .41**), negatively with anxiety (M9, –.16*), and positively with a number of learning activities involving open-ended language use in MSQ Part II and the end-of-training student learning activities questionnaires, e.g., finds open-ended discussion useful .13*. Similarly, AFF intrinsic (self-report) correlates (inversely) with anxiety (general discomfort –.45***) and (directly) with MSQ intrinsic (.38*) and extrinsic (.41*), Modern Language Aptitude Test (MLAT) IV (grammar sensitivity, .24**), as well as end-of-training speaking and reading proficiencies (.28* and .33**, respectively).

MSQ extrinsic motivation

MSQ extrinsic correlates alone (i.e., without MSQ intrinsic) with scales from the AFF of low anxiety about tests (–.45*) and lack of general discomfort (–.39*). In addition, it is correlated with Myers-Briggs Type Indicator (MBTI) extroversion (–.16*), perceiving (.17*), and MLAT I (auditory number recognition, .19*). Note that in other studies, extroversion and perceiving have tended to correlate with measures of self-confidence (e.g., Ehrman, 1994). The pattern of correlations may thus suggest that M8 extrinsic sub-items from the MSQ express some form of self-confidence.

Because the self-report intrinsic measures appear to include correlations with general motivation items and with a variety of learning preferences and because AFF intrinsic correlates with the MSQ motivation items, whereas AFF extrinsic does not, the pattern of correlations for the intrinsic measures may indicate that it represents the more generic motivation variable, whereas extrinsic motivation appears to be more related to personality dispositions.

AFF intrinsic and AFF extrinsic

Both of these correlate with thin ego boundaries on the Hartmann Boundary Questionnaire (HBQ), especially preference for blurred edges in images (MSQ intrinsic and edges .18**), with MBTI intuition (MSQ extrinsic and intuition .18**), and with MSQ self-efficacy (extrinsic and M1 .19**, intrinsic and M3 .28***) and AFF self-efficacy (beliefs about self .40*** and .58***, respectively). Both AFF intrinsic and AFF extrinsic correlate negatively with AFF anxiety and negative attitude variables (e.g., AFF extrinsic and negative motivation items –.40***, AFF intrinsic and negative motivation items –.85***).

---

[2] The distinction between intrinsic and extrinsic motivation is obscured in factor analysis of AFF and in a number of the correlations for AFF and MSQ, which largely overlap.

The distinction between the a priori AFF extrinsic and AFF intrinsic scales may be artificial; this is confirmed by a factor analysis, which found only one motivation factor in the AFF that included most of the items from both a priori scales.

Post-hoc teacher ratings

These ratings suggest that students who are perceived by their teachers as better learners are also perceived as intrinsically motivated by those teachers (teacher-rating groups with teacher intrinsic .43**). Being perceived as extrinsically motivated is less strongly linked with perception as a good student (teacher rating groups with teacher extrinsic .25*). This phenomenon may be a function of teachers' experiencing these students as personally involved with them, their language, and their culture; we tend to value those whom we experience as valuing us.

In actual fact, end-of-training success correlates only with teacher ratings of specific forms of *extrinsic* motivation. Correlations are with the following: "get an award" with end-of-training reading proficiency (EOTR) and end-of-training speaking proficiency (EOTS) .11*; be the best with EOTR .16**; and EOTR .12**; higher pay with EOTS .11*, get off language probation with EOTR .15** and EOTS .16**, and *not* with teacher-ratings of any form of *intrinsic* motivation.[3]

Teacher ratings of observed anxiety are strongly and inversely correlated with MSQ M4 (−.68*) and M6 (−.76**). Although the number of observations (10) is very low, the strength of the correlations suggests that they are likely to hold as the N goes up.

Motivation variables

M4, M5, and M6 on the MSQ correlate with personality variables in ways I found surprising. Self-reported motivation M4 correlates with MBTI thinking (.20***) and with thinking and judging subscales on the Type Differentiation Indicator (TDI, the long version of the MBTI), e.g., *reasonable* versus compassionate .24***. I interpret these links as indicating some need for control. In a similar vein, M4 and M5 in particular correlate at about −.15** with thick boundaries on the Hartmann Boundary Questionnaire (HBQ), which can indicate need for control and low tolerance for ambiguity (see Ehrman, 1993). In contrast, the composite MSQ extrinsic and intrinsic scales correlate with extroversion .16*, intuition .18**, perceiving .17*, and thin boundaries on the HBQ .16*, suggesting greater tolerance for ambiguity. Do M4-M6 on the one hand and the MSQ extrinsic and intrinsic scales indicate two different entities, where M4-M6 indicate control needs and less

---

[3]   Post-hoc teacher perceptions of being a good student correlate considerably more highly with actual end-of-training ratings than do their motivation ratings, so these data all probably tell us considerably more about our teachers and student-teacher relations than about the students alone, but this is the topic of another paper.

tolerance of ambiguity, whereas MSQ extrinsic and intrinsic composite scales indicate more tolerance for ambiguity?

A look at the classroom activities associated with each set of variables may shed more light on this question. M4 and M5 have considerable overlap in their correlations with other variables (M6 has relatively few correlations). M4 and M5 are generally linked with preferences for relatively *open-ended activities*. MSQ extrinsic has few correlations, but MSQ intrinsic is also related to relatively open-ended learning activities as well. On the other hand, M4, M5, and MSQ intrinsic are also intercorrelated but at a low level (ca. .20**). If they are different as suggested above from the personality correlations, the difference may not affect the classroom. Still, this pattern of correlation in different directions for the two sets of MSQ motivation items warrants further investigation.

SELF-EFFICACY

Immediately striking is the degree to which a sense of self-efficacy as measured by rather simple statements of self-confidence in one's learning ability (M1, M2, M3) correlates consistently with EOTS and EOTR, though not very strongly (.20s* for MSQ measures; .29** for AFF beliefs about self, for both EOTS and EOTR). The highest correlation is between favorable comparison of self with other FSI learners (M2) and EOTR .30*: thus a context-specific self-confidence may be more related to learning success than more generalized expectations.

Students who express self-confidence in items M1-M3 tend to do well on the MLAT. The Index Score correlations are in the 30s** and 40s**. The strongest part score correlation is with MLAT IV, grammar sensitivity, .36. One can hardly help wondering if people who have the skills that permit them to do well on tests like the MLAT are likely to feel high self-efficacy in an academic situation because they have already had a record of success, or are they successful because of their self-confidence, or some reciprocal combination of the two? Realistic self-assessment of one's own abilities may be a moderating variable in other relationships between individual variables and success in learning.

Like the MSQ motivation items, all the self-confidence items M1-M3 correlate with an expressed preference at the beginning of training for relatively open-ended learning activities and broad exposure to the language, e.g., M1 .23*** with reading texts with unfamiliar words and phrases. (Note that these findings contrast with the results for anxiety discussed below.)

General belief in oneself as a learner correlates inconsistently with motivation variables: the MSQ self-confidence items M1, M2 do not correlate with the general motivation variables M4-M6 at all. Specific expectation that one will do well in this language (M3), on the other hand, does appear to relate to motivation at a low level (M4 .22***, M5 .25***, M6 .16**).

MBTI intuition has a correlation with belief in one's ability (M1 .27***, M3 .18**), as do some of the TDI subscales that indicate relative open-endedness (e.g., M1 with pragmatic-*intellectual* .33***) and HBQ thin boundaries (HBQ Total and M1 .16*), possibly indicating a link between self-confidence and receptivity. (Other studies have shown a link between these personality constructs and the same kind of preference for open-ended activities as we have seen for motivation and self-efficacy; see Ehrman, 1994b.)

AFF and MSQ self-efficacy and self-reported anxiety are moderately negatively correlated (–30s and 40s**). The fact that the correlations are not higher indicates that they may be independent factors, so that one can be both self-confident and anxious.

ANXIETY

Self-reported anxiety on MSQ M9 (general anxiety about language learning) is negatively correlated with EOT ratings (EOTR –.25**, EOTS –.20*). It is also negatively correlated with the MLAT in the .20s, e.g., Index –.25**. At a low level, M9 correlates with MBTI feeling (.17**) and with thinner boundaries (HBQ Total .17**). This is the downside of thin boundaries, whereas we have seen above the upside in the relationship between motivation and self-efficacy on the one hand and greater HBQ openness on the other. Among the learning activities in the MSQ, high anxious students on M9 tend to endorse relatively limited classroom activities and methods (e.g., closely following syllabus .14*) and reject open-ended ones (e.g., role-plays –.20***). Such limitation of risk may also limit learning opportunities.

MSQ M10 (anxiety about speaking in class) shows a similar pattern, negatively correlating with M1 and M3–5 around –.20** and negatively correlating with open-ended activities or those that require guessing (e.g., –.23*** with teacher makes explanations in the target language). M9 and M10 are intercorrelated at .59***.

An anomalous variable

High scores on one AFF variable, whose items and scoring are comparable to other anxiety items on AFF, have shown an anomalous pattern. I have called this variable "public performance"; it refers to feelings about oral production in the classroom. Public performance varies *inversely* with other forms of anxiety and appears to serve more as another measure of self-efficacy for the FSI population (it generally covaries with self-efficacy measures, e.g., AFF beliefs about self .50***). I have also interpreted it as an indication of facilitating anxiety, because of the fact that it is phrased and structured like more conventionally behaving anxiety variables, which clearly indicate debilitating anxiety, and yet it is consistently associated both with EOT success (EOTR .26**, EOTS .23**) and negatively with other indications of negative affect (e.g., error correction anxiety –.57** and overall negative affect –.63**).

MSQ item M10 was intended as an analog of the AFF public performance scale. However, unlike public performance, it correlates with one of the same items as M9 and in the same pattern. It differs markedly from M9 in that it has no correlates with the MLAT but instead with a considerable number of the MBTI scales and subscales, so that it is perhaps partly an indicator of a certain personality profile, somewhat as we saw above for extrinsic motivation. More specifically, students who indicate anxiety about speaking in class on the MSQ have a very slight tendency to be more introverted (.16*) and feeling (.13*), and they indicate certain kinds of thin boundaries (e.g., sensitivity .14*). Thin boundaries in turn correlate with introversion, feeling, and MBTI/TDI anxiety indicators.

Teacher post-hoc ratings of anxiety

These ratings correlate with little, even self-reported anxiety on the AFF and the MSQ. One of the few correlates was with a variant of teacher overall rating of the student, where there was a link between teacher-perceived weakness as a student and teacher-rated anxiety (.31***). As noted above, teacher ratings of anxiety also correlate negatively with MSQ motivation items M4 and M6. The self-report anxiety variables have proved to be more reliable and relevant to proficiency outcomes than teacher post-hoc ratings.

Negative items

The negatively phrased items in AFF (e.g., "I find language study depressing") were extracted to make an additional set of subscales: negative motivation, negatively phrased anxiety items, and a negative total. This negative item total was found to covary with self-reported anxiety about error correction (.37***), anxiety about maintaining self-esteem (.35***), test anxiety (.21**), and anxiety about competition with classmates (.35***), and with general discomfort with language learning (.16*) on the AFF. The negative item total is inversely correlated with AFF public performance (−.63***) beliefs about self (−.22**), MSQ M5 (motivation related to career), EOTR (−.23**), and EOTS (−.26**).

WHAT'S INTERESTING: DISCUSSION OF FINDINGS

Main findings are summarized in Table 4 and discussed below.

Table 4: Patterns of findings

MOTIVATION

Self-reported *intrinsic* motivation correlates with general motivation, self-efficacy, open-ended learning, MLAT grammatical sensitivity, end-of-training speaking and reading proficiency, and negatively with anxiety.

Self-reported *extrinsic* motivation correlates with extroversion, perceiving, MLAT number recognition, and negatively with anxiety, but does not correlate with general motivation.

Intrinsic motivation may represent the more generic variable.

MSQ extrinsic motivation may be another expression of personality-based self-confidence.

Both AFF extrinsic and intrinsic are related to thin ego boundaries, intuition, self-efficacy, and negatively with anxiety and negatively phrased items.

The intrinsic and extrinsic motivation distinction may be artificial for the FSI sample.

Teachers tend to perceive better learners as more intrinsically motivated, though actual higher end-of-training scores are correlated with teacher ratings of extrinsic motivation.

MSQ M4, M5, and M6 correlate with thick boundaries, MBTI thinking, judging subscales, and apparent low tolerance for ambiguity, whereas MSQ intrinsic and extrinsic and AFF motivation variables correlate with thin boundaries, MBTI introversion, intuition, and perceiving, thus tolerance for ambiguity.

The contrast in the above two sets of findings presents a puzzle about whether there are two motivation constructs in the MSQ.

All motivation variables tend to correlate with preference for open-ended classroom activities.

SELF-EFFICACY

Correlation with end-of-training reading and end-of-training speaking proficiency.

Also correlated with the MLAT, especially Part IV (Words in Sentences).

M1, M2, M3 correlate with preference for open-ended learning activities.

Only specific self-efficacy (expect to do well in this language) on the MSQ is related to motivation.

continued...

Table 4: Patterns of findings (cont.)

MSQ self-efficacy is linked with MBTI intuition and HBQ thin boundaries.

Self-efficacy and anxiety are negatively correlated at a moderate level.

ANXIETY

Anxiety is negatively correlated with end-of-training ratings in speaking and reading and with the MLAT.

Anxiety is correlated with MBTI introversion and feeling and with HBQ thin boundaries.

Anxious students tend to endorse activities that limit risk (and may limit learning, too).

One AFF anxiety variable, "Public Performance," behaves oppositely from the other anxiety variables and more like an indicator of self-efficacy.

On the other hand, MSQ item M10, also about speaking in class, behaves like other anxiety variables.

Teacher post-hoc anxiety ratings correlate with teacher perceptions of worse performance and negatively with self-reported motivation on the MSQ. However, they are unrelated to end-of-training proficiency.

Endorsement of negatively phrased items also correlates with anxiety and negatively with self-efficacy and motivation indicators.

MOTIVATION

An interesting question is raised by the fact that students perceive themselves as intrinsically motivated, whereas external observers (and evidence from other individual difference measures) suggest more extrinsic motivation. Perhaps this is an effect of student perceptions of the social desirability of being intrinsically motivated, or at least motivated by a desire to learn the language for more than simply instrumental reasons. It may be, of course, that they frequently enter training with relatively intrinsic motivations that become overshadowed by the pressures of the proficiency test and the assignment-related rewards and sanctions that depend on the test.

The distinction between extrinsic and intrinsic motivation (and perhaps instrumental vs. integrative) does not seem very robust for the FSI population. Perhaps this is an effect of self-selection: having chosen a foreign affairs career (and in the case of foreign service officers, going through the grueling selection process) might already imply some underlying intrinsic motivation related to foreign affairs, so there would be relatively little variation among FSI students. On the other hand, the overwhelmingly powerful instrumental impetus of career and impending assignment militate in the opposite direction, but for the same people. In general, training staff at FSI observe that for most students there is a visible "burnout" and reduced intrinsic motivation by about the third FSI language. The test and need to use the language as a work tool during the upcoming assignment come to take on much more motivational weight. This has not been tested formally, however. It may also be that the same students learn enough to be functional but are less receptive to influence from later target languages and cultures that might affect their identities or world views — that is, they may maintain thicker boundaries. This, too, remains to be tested.

The contradictory findings for the two sets of MSQ motivation variables (M4–6 vs. MSQ intrinsic and extrinsic) based on their correlations with personality variables may indicate two different constructs. As noted above, this is not clear, and additional evidence from other correlations does not answer the question.

Motivation is generally correlated negatively with anxiety on the questionnaires. However, the intensity of motivation (usually extrinsic) is clearly a two-edged sword in practice, because it can lead to increased anxiety, stress, and overwork, especially when a student is not meeting his or her own expectations of success.

We have seen that teachers tend to perceive the students they rate as intrinsically motivated as more successful students. Could it be that they are misinterpreting general motivation (both extrinsic and intrinsic, instrumental and integrative) as liking for their language and culture? Or could it be that instrumental motivation leads to both exposure to the language, culture, and people and to a certain level of learning success, and these in turn lead to intrinsic motivation in the student?

SELF-EFFICACY

The findings for the self-efficacy measures suggest a "Matthew Effect" (to those who have shall be given more), to wit, to the self-confident tend to go the higher MLAT scores and the EOT ratings. I suggest some possible reasons: doing well on the higher MLAT (and in previous language study) may build self-confidence, or self-confidence promotes effective use of one's cognitive resources, or, alternatively, with a sense of self-efficacy comes a realistic self-appraisal of one's ability to cope with the task at hand.

Personality variables (MBTI intuition, relatively thinner boundaries on the HBQ) indicate a connection between openness to the new and a sense of self-efficacy as a language learner. This link is independent of the kind of surgency usually reported for extroversion in much of the personality literature (Myers and McCaulley, 1985).

There is a considerable inverse relationship between self-efficacy and anxiety, but not a completely complementary distribution. Self-efficacy may provide not only a realistic assessment of one's coping resources, it may also enhance the learner's access to these. Contrariwise, anxiety, working somewhat independently, acts to reduce the availability of cognitive and other learning resources. However, the two do not necessarily cancel each other out, so there may be either a net effect in one or the other direction or an oscillation between states of optimism and anxiety.

ANXIETY/NEGATIVE AFFECT

In general, anxiety is seen to be debilitating in relation to end-of-training performance and to lead to students restricting their own options through preference for closed-ended training. The one exception for this population seems to be the AFF public performance anxiety variable, which runs counter to the other AFF anxiety scales, to the usual findings for university students, and to MSQ M9 and M10, as well. This variable seems to be more a self-efficacy measure.

Post-hoc teacher ratings of student anxiety provide little information, which is somewhat surprising. Along with the findings about teacher ratings for motivation, this finding suggests that there are some interesting dynamics that are beyond the scope of this presentation but may illuminate teacher-student interrelations at FSI in useful ways. Students who are perceived as anxious are also perceived as less successful, though there is *no* relation between faculty-rated anxiety and actual end-of-training scores.

The superiority of self-report ratings on motivation and anxiety to teacher ratings also raises interesting questions. Is the difficulty a lack of consistency among faculty raters? Would some rater training for all interviewees have made a difference? (Interviewers, who took the data from staff, were trained.) Is it the case, in fact, that teachers are subjectively swayed by their feelings about their students?

CONCLUDING STATEMENT

It is interesting that so much can come from a single question on the MSQ, e.g., M1 or M4 or M9, that addresses the domain covered by a set of questions in the AFF. It is possible that the MSQ will do much of what the AFF tries to do, but more simply. The two really useful features in the AFF that it lacks are the negative item subscales and the "Public Performance" scale. The former provides valuable additional information that can help us understand our almost uniformly highly motivated students at FSI; the second may indicate some facilitating anxiety that the MSQ does not tap.

This paper is intended as a preliminary report on affective dimensions in the FSI study. It is therefore not surprising that interesting questions are raised in these findings about the nature of motivation constructs, particularly what is meant by extrinsic and intrinsic motivation. We have seen that they do not seem to mean the same thing to teachers and students (or else the two groups perceive student motivation in different ways), and we have seen different correlation patterns with other individual difference variables. Teacher-perceived extrinsic motivation and student-perceived intrinsic motivation are linked to end-of-training proficiency outcomes. We need further investigation of the interesting questions raised by this phenomenon.

These findings also suggest that motivation is more situation or person-and-situation specific than our instrumentation and general constructs can show. Ideally, these instruments would be analyzed together with qualitative case information on the respondents, so that respondent interpretations of the items would shed light on some of the contradictory or anomalous patterns that appear in the present findings.

Affective variables, together with personality variables like those in the MBTI or the Hartmann Boundary Questionnaire, tend to have relatively low correlations with outcome variables like end-of-training proficiency. However, they probably play a substantial role in the success of individual learners because of their impact on the mobilization of cognitive and interpersonal resources.

Furthermore, they affect the efficiency of learning because they mediate the match among learning, teacher, and program structure, as described in Ehrman (in press). A good match promotes efficiency. Just enough mismatch, like just enough anxiety or arousal, is needed to challenge the learner but not so much that motivation and self-efficacy are reduced and energy is wasted that could be applied to learning.

APPENDIX: INSTRUMENTATION IN THIS PAPER

Affective Survey
(Ehrman and Oxford, 1991)

The Affective Survey is a 114-item instrument developed by Ehrman and Oxford (1991) with certain general ideas and in some instances adapted items from a variety of surveys and scales by Gardner (1985b), Campbell (1987), Horwitz (1985), Horwitz et al. (1986), and others. The authors recognized that no single survey or scale covered all the important affective (emotional and motivational) areas related to language learning success. The Affective Survey contains three parts: motivation (extrinsic, intrinsic, desire to use the language, and effort), beliefs about self as a language learner, and anxiety (as related to speaking in class, language use with native speakers, making errors, comprehension, self-esteem, competition, tests, outcomes, and general comfort or discomfort with language learning). The Affective Survey also has the option of a "negativity scale," which indicates how often a person agrees with negatively worded items about motivation and anxiety. The Cronbach alpha internal consistency reliability for the Affective Survey is .74, and the standardized item alpha is .82.

The Hartmann Boundary Questionnaire (HBQ)
(Hartmann, 1991)

The HBQ was developed for research with sleep disorders and nightmares, using a psychoanalytic theoretical base. It is intended to examine the degree to which individuals separate aspects of their mental, interpersonal, and external experience through "thick" or "thin" psychological boundaries. Its 146 items address the following dimensions: sleep/dreams/wakefulness, unusual experiences, boundaries among thoughts/feelings/moods, impressions of childhood/adolescence/adulthood, interpersonal distance/openness/closeness, physical and emotional sensitivity, preference for neatness, preference for clear lines, opinions about children/adolescents/adults, opinions about lines of authority, opinions about boundaries among groups/peoples/nations, opinions about abstract concepts, plus a total score for all twelve of the above scales. Hartmann found women and younger people to score consistently "thinner" than men and older people. Cronbach alpha reliability for the HBQ is .93, and theta reliabilities for subscales are .57–.92 (Hartmann, 1991).

The Language Learning Motivation and Strategies Questionnaire (MSQ)
(Christensen and Ehrman, 1993)

In Part I, 10 items address motivation, self-efficacy, and anxiety. Part II consists of four items addressing various learning and teaching techniques that are used in FSI classrooms. Many of the items in Part II were designed to match the Student Learning Activities Questionnaires (see below) which are used at the end of training. The items are Likert-scaled. This paper is the first report on the use of the MSQ.

The Myers-Briggs Type Indicator (MBTI), Form G
(Myers and McCaulley, 1985)

This instrument is a 126-item, forced-choice, normative, self-report questionnaire designed to reveal basic personality preferences on four scales: extroversion-introversion (whether the person obtains energy [externally or internally]); sensing-intuition (whether the person is concrete/sequential or abstract/random); thinking-feeling (whether the person makes decisions based on objective logic or subjective values); and judging-perceiving (whether the person needs rapid closure or prefers a flexible life). Internal consistency split-half reliabilities average .87, and test-retest reliabilities are .70–.85 (Myers and McCaulley, 1985). Concurrent validity is documented with personality, vocational preference, educational style, and management style (.40–.77). Construct validity is supported by many studies of occupational preferences and creativity.

The Type Differentiation Indicator (TDI)
(Saunders, 1989)

The TDI is a scoring system for a longer and more intricate 290-item form (MBTI Form J) that provides data on the following subscales for each of the four MBTI dimensions: extroversion-introversion (gregarious-intimate, enthusiastic-quiet, initiator-receptor, expressive-contained, auditory-visual); sensing-intuition (concrete-abstract, realistic-imaginative, pragmatic-intellectual, experiential-theoretical, traditional-original); thinking-feeling (critical-accepting, tough-tender, questioning-accommodating, reasonable-compassionate, logical-affective); and judging-perceiving (stress avoider-polyactive, systematic-casual, schedules-spontaneous, playful-open-ended, methodical-emergent). The TDI includes seven additional scales indicating a sense of overall comfort and confidence versus discomfort and anxiety (guarded-optimistic, defiant-compliant, carefree-worried, decisive-ambivalent, intrepid-inhibited, leader-follower, proactive-distractible), plus a composite of these called "strain." Each of these comfort-discomfort subscales also loads on one of the four type dimensions, e.g., proactive-distractive is also a judging-perceiving subscale. There are also scales for type-scale consistency and comfort-scale consistency. Reliability of 23 of the 27 TDI subscales is greater than .50, an acceptable result given the brevity of the subscales (Saunders, 1989).

The Modern Language Aptitude Test (MLAT)
(Carroll and Sapon, 1959)

This is the classic language aptitude test, with 146 items. The manual describes its five parts: I – number learning (memory, auditory alertness); II – phonetic script (association of sounds and symbols); III – spelling clues (English vocabulary, association of sounds and symbols); IV – words in sentences (grammatical structure in English); and V – paired associates (memorizing words). The MLAT was correlated .67 with the Primary Mental Abilities Test (Wesche, Edwards, and Wells, 1982), suggesting a strong general intelligence factor operating in the MLAT. Split-half reliabilities for the MLAT are .92–.97, depending on the grade or age. For college students, validity coefficients are .18–.69 for the long form of the MLAT and .21–.68 for the short form. For adult students in intensive language programs, validity coefficients are .27–.73 for the long form and .26–.69 for the short form (Caroll and Sapon, 1959). In this sample, almost all (95%) of the MLAT scores were current, i.e., within the last 3 years. This study used the long form.

Measures of Student Language Proficiency

At the end of training, FSI students are given proficiency assessments resulting in ratings ranging from 0 to 5 for speaking (including interactive listening comprehension) and for reading. For example, R–3 means reading proficiency level 3; S–2 means speaking proficiency level 2. The ratings are equivalent to the guidelines of the Interagency Language Roundtable/American Council on the Teaching of Foreign Languages (ILR/ACTFL) that originated at FSI and have been developed over the years by government agencies. (These guidelines are detailed by Omaggio, 1986.) FSI usually aims at end-of-training proficiency ratings of S–3 R–3 for full-time training, comparable to ILR/ACTFL Advanced Proficiency. Reliability studies have shown that government agencies have high interrater reliability for proficiency ratings within a given agency, but that the standards are not always the same at every agency; thus raters at different government agencies do not have as high an interrater reliability as raters at the same agency. Proficiency ratings are thus considered reliable indicators of the level of language performance of an individual student within an agency (Clark, 1986). "Plus" scores (e.g., indicating proficiency between S–2 and S–3) were coded as 0.5; thus, for example, a score of S–2+ was coded 2.5.

Faculty Rating Questionnaire

After training was complete, faculty were asked to rate students on effort, observed aptitude, motivation, anxiety, and overall quality of a student relative to other FSI students. Data were collected by interview in order to get a rich texture of comments as well as quantitative data. In order to achieve reliability, interviewers were trained and asked to follow the format of the questionnaire. Although faculty ratings are not the focus of this paper, they are referred to throughout.

Student Learning Activities Questionnaires

At the end of training, each student in the study was asked to complete two questionnaires: CLASSACT (Ehrman and Jackson, 1992) on relative usefulness of a fairly detailed list of classroom activities (Likert scaled 1–3) and SELFACT (Hart-Gonzalez and Ehrman, 1992) on relative usefulness (1–3) of their own study activities and estimated time per week devoted to each. These questionnaires are used here for the first time. Because completion at end of training was voluntary and students were very busy with preparations for departure, the return rate was low, and N's for a number of the items are not adequate for analysis. This and other studies using these two questionnaires are part of their validation. When there are sufficient cases, they will be subjected to reliability analysis and factor analysis.

NOTE

This appendix is taken largely from Ehrman and Oxford (1995) and Oxford and Ehrman (1995).

Mayumi Okada
Hiroshima, Japan

Rebecca L. Oxford
The University of Alabama

Suzuna Abo
Hobart and William Smith College

CHAPTER 5

NOT ALL ALIKE: MOTIVATION AND LEARNING STRATEGIES AMONG STUDENTS OF JAPANESE AND SPANISH IN AN EXPLORATORY STUDY

ABSTRACT

A group of 72 students around the US participated in an exploratory study of learning strategy use and motivation in foreign language learning. Each of these students was studying either Japanese or Spanish at the college level. Observation was made of the strategy frequencies. The study also examined degrees and types of motivation exhibited by these students. Based on the strategy and motivation results, the authors provided implications for instruction.

INTRODUCTION

Language learning is difficult. People try one technique after another, seeking the most effective one for them. Types of learning styles and the learning strategies (techniques) used for language development vary from culture to culture. Even within the same culture, strategy use may differ, especially for people learning different languages (Oxford, Hollaway, and Murillo, 1992; Reid, 1987, 1995). There are thousands of languages in the world. Some of the strategies used can be expected to differ from one language to another if the levels of difficulty of the languages are not the same, as in Japanese and Spanish learned by native English speakers. Moreover, motivation must often be higher when one tries to learn more difficult languages, because greater persistence and determination are needed to cope with the stress of a difficult situation.

This study helps determine if language specificity exists in learning strategy use. This investigation also assesses the degree to which motivation is related to the use of learning strategies in language learning at two levels of difficulty. We chose to

Okada, Mayumi, Oxford, Rebecca, & Abo, Suzuna (1996). Not all alike: Motivation and learning strategies among students of Japanese and Spanish in an exploratory study. In Rebecca Oxford (Ed.), *Language Learning Motivation: Pathways to the New Century.* (Technical Report #11) (pp. 105–119). Honolulu: University of Hawai'i, Second Language Teaching & Curriculum Center.

compare (1) a language at the easiest level (ACTFL/ETS Level I) for native English speakers to learn with (2) a language at the most difficult level (Level IV) for native English speakers. Therefore, we selected Spanish, a Level I language, and Japanese, a Level IV language. The base language of all the participants was English.

RESEARCH REVIEW

This research review concerns language learning motivation and learning strategies, the two primary variables in this study.

MOTIVATION

Motivation is important to language learning because it helps determine the extent of involvement in learning. High motivation spurs learners to interact with native speakers of the language, which in turn increases the amount of input learners receive (Krashen, 1982; Scarcella and Oxford, 1992). Motivation is linked with high-frequency use of language learning strategies (Oxford and Nyikos, 1989). Motivation helps students maintain their language ability after students leave the classroom (Gardner, Lalonde, Moorcroft, and Evers, 1985).

Motivation encourages greater overall effort on the part of learners and thus greater success in language performance, both in general terms (Clément, Major, Gardner, and Smythe, 1977; Gardner, 1985b; Samimy and Tabuse, 1991) and in specific skill areas (Genesee, 1978; Genesee and Hamayan, 1980; Tucker, Hamayan, and Genesee, 1976). Yet the relationship between motivation and language performance is not identical for all languages in a study by Youssef (1984); results show a far stronger link for learners of French and German than for learners of Spanish.

One comprehensive definition of language learning motivation is that of Crookes and Schmidt (1991), who state that such motivation consists of seven elements: (1) interest, (2) relevance, (3) expectancy of success or failure, (4) belief in forthcoming rewards, (5) decision to be involved, (6) persistence, and (7) high activity level. These components are detailed elsewhere in this volume, especially in Chapters 2 and 6. Attitudes and beliefs clearly affect behaviors within this definition of language learning motivation. A teacher who overcorrects the student can lower the expectation of success and destroy the possibility of a reward, thus reducing the student's willingness to pay attention or to persist in language learning. If the language activities are perceived as irrelevant or uninteresting, the level of activity and engagement will drop. Any negative attitude toward the target language or culture can also be detrimental to engagement, persistence, or activity level.

A well-known social psychological distinction in discussions of language learning motivation occurs between *integrative* motivation and *instrumental* motivation (Gardner, 1985b; Gardner and Lambert, 1959, 1972). The first, integrative, refers to the desire to learn the language out of sheer interest or to become closer to the target culture, though not necessarily integrating fully with that culture. The integrative motive is the linchpin of the Socio-Educational Model of Gardner and his colleagues. The second motivational type, instrumental, concerns the desire to learn the language as a means of improving one's status (e.g., job, academic requirements). This motivation, while mentioned by Gardner and his co-researchers, is not a strong part of the Socio-Educational Model.

Oxford (1992) states that these two motivational orientations, although helpful, were insufficient to explain the wide array of reasons that students learn languages; see Chapter 6 for information. Likewise, Dörnyei (1990a) shows that instrumental and integrative motivations were less influential in language achievement than was another aspect of motivation, the general need for achievement. In addition, Au (1988), Crookes and Schmidt (1991), Horwitz (1990), and Oller (1981) also call for a reevaluation of the significance of the integrative-instrumental split.

Oxford and Shearin (1994) offer an expanded framework of language learning motivation, drawing upon theories such as need for achievement, equity, self-efficacy, locus of control, expectancy-value, reinforcement, mastery learning, and developmental cognition. Dörnyei (1994a) emphasizes the need for looking at language learning motivation in a broader fashion. Tremblay and Gardner (1995) respond by expanding the Socio-Educational model to include many of the variables that were heretofore missing, such as self-efficacy and attributions.

Empirical research by Ehrman and Oxford (1995) used a broad-scope instrument, the Affective Survey, to assess motivation. In that study, motivation was correlated from the .20s to the high .50s with language learning strategy use. The highest correlation was between motivation and cognitive strategy use.

LANGUAGE LEARNING STRATEGIES

Language learning strategies are the often conscious steps or behaviors used by language learners to enhance their own learning (Oxford, 1990b, 1993). These strategies help learners take in aspects of the language, store them in long-term memory, and use them when needed. Research indicates that learners at all levels of proficiency use language learning strategies, but some learners are relatively unaware of the strategies they use. More proficient learners often use a wider range of strategies and consciously employ these in a more organized, better tailored way (O'Malley and Chamot, 1990; Wenden and Rubin, 1987).

Specifically, more effective learners use strategies that are linked both to their own general learning styles (see Ehrman and Oxford, 1990; Oxford, Ehrman, and Lavine, 1991) and to the language task at hand (O'Malley and Chamot, 1990). Previous research shows that learning style (for example, visual, auditory, hands-on; reflective, impulsive; extroverted, introverted; closure-oriented, open; intuitive-random, concrete-sequential; analytic, global) frequently influences the kinds of learning strategies students choose (Ehrman and Oxford, 1989, 1990). Research also suggests that language learning aptitude might be related to learning strategy use, as well as to learning styles (Oxford, 1990b).

Investigations of strategy use show that successful language learners use a variety of strategies to become more self-directed and improve their performance (Cohen, 1990; Nyikos, 1987; O'Malley and Chamot, 1990; Oxford, 1989, 1990a, 1990b, 1993; Wenden and Rubin, 1987). Direct, significant relationships between learning strategy use and language performance have been found, with the latter measured through course grades, achievement or proficiency scores, placement results, teacher ratings, and student self-ratings (see summary in Oxford and Burry-Stock, 1995).

Strategy use has also been shown to relate to gender. Across many studies, females are often shown to use more strategies at higher levels than males, regardless of the cultural background involved. The reason for this remains to be discovered, but it might relate to socialization (by schools, families, or general society) as well as possible physical differences in brain functioning (see Oxford, 1995).

Learning strategy use has been assessed in many different ways. Student diaries, think-aloud procedures while doing a language task, group and individual interviews, computer tracking, and questionnaires are among the many modes of strategy assessment. The current study uses a language learning strategy questionnaire.

HYPOTHESES

Three hypotheses guide this study:

1. Learners of Japanese are more motivated than learners of Spanish.

2. Learners of Japanese show more frequent use of a wider range of strategies than do learners of Spanish.

3. Significant correlations exist between motivation and strategy use for each language group.

METHODS

SAMPLE

The 72 participants — 36 Japanese learners and 36 Spanish learners — completed both instruments and therefore comprised the final sample. Subjects were chosen exclusively from students whose first language is English. They were all college students at levels ranging from Japanese 101 to 201 (with only two fourth-year Japanese students included) and from Spanish 101 to 201. It was expected that the two fourth-year Japanese students could not, statistically speaking, alter the trend of the Japanese 101–201 data in any meaningful way.

There were two science majors, 14 business majors, 13 humanities majors, and one premedical major among the learners of Japanese; and two science majors, 10 business majors, 18 humanities majors, and two premedical majors among the learners of Spanish. The groups differed mainly in that the Japanese group had a few more business majors, while the Spanish group had a few more humanities majors, but this difference did not seem to be crucial.

Most Japanese learners in this investigation were from the University of Alabama. Others came from Arkansas State University, Slippery Rock State University (PA), King's College (PA), Alma College (MI), and Wesleyan College (GA). The Spanish learners were from the University of Alabama and King's College. All the Japanese learners used *Japanese: The Spoken Language (JSL)* by Jorden and Noda (1987) as their textbook, and most of the Japanese instructors were trained by Dr. Eleanor Jorden. The Spanish learners used two texts, *Sabías que...?* (Van Patten, Lee, Ballman and Dvorak, 1992) and *Pasajes* (Bretz, Dvorak, and Kirschner, 1992), and the instructors conducted the classes using the Natural Approach.

INSTRUMENTATION

Two instruments were used: the Modified Strategy Inventory for Language Learning (SILL, Oxford, 1990a) and the Modified Affective Survey (AFF, Ehrman and Oxford, 1991).

Strategy Inventory for Language Learning

The SILL was developed by Rebecca Oxford (1990a). In this study, Version 5.1 (for English speakers learning foreign languages) was used. The SILL is a questionnaire for assessing students' frequency of use of learning strategies and consists of strategy descriptions to be answered on a Likert scale of 1 to 5, according to the frequency of use by the respondent. The points on the scale are (1) never or almost never true of me, (2) generally not true of me, (3) somewhat true of me, (4) generally true of me, and (5) always or almost always true of me. The SILL is self-scoring and provides immediate feedback to learners.

Version 5.1 of the SILL has 80 items. However, for the purposes of this study the SILL was modified by eliminating the reading and writing items, because *JSL* focuses almost solely on speaking and listening and because the Natural Approach, particularly in years one and two (101 through 202 at most institutions) emphasizes oral communication skills. Nine items were omitted, leaving a total of 71 strategies measured. The resulting modified questionnaire had 15 items reflecting memory strategies, 18 for cognitive strategies, 7 for compensation strategies, 16 for metacognitive strategies, 7 for affective strategies, and 8 for social strategies.

The SILL for English speakers learning foreign languages is based on six general categories of strategies: memory, cognitive, metacognitive, compensation, affective, and social. Each SILL packet consists of directions to the student, a sample item, and the questionnaire itself, followed by a scoring worksheet and a strategy graph sheet for the student to use.

Cronbach alpha internal consistency reliability of the whole, unmodified SILL (Version 5.1) ranges from .89 to .92 with an average of .91 in studies worldwide (Oxford and Burry-Stock, 1995). Studies of reliability for this version contained 236, 337, and 321 students respectively. In terms of validity, the SILL is either a predictor or a correlate, depending on the research design, of language performance (grades, tests, teacher-ratings, and self-ratings) in many studies at the level of .40 to .80 (Oxford and Burry-Stock, 1995). Validity is further supported by the fact that strategies on the SILL correlate with learning styles at a range of .47 to .87 using the Learning Style Profile and the Myers-Briggs Type Indicator (Oxford and Burry-Stock, 1995). Results of the SILL are not faked, according to a social-desirability study by Yang (1992) with 505 students.

Affective Survey

The Affective Survey is a 118-item, six-point Likert-scaled instrument developed by Madeline Ehrman and Rebecca Oxford (1991) with some ideas and item types adapted from a variety of scales by Robert Gardner (1985b), Elaine Horwitz (1990), and others. Ehrman and Oxford recognized that no single scale covered all the important affective (emotional and motivational) areas related to language learning success and that it would be necessary to construct a more comprehensive scale, such as the AFF. This survey contains three parts: motivation (extrinsic, intrinsic, desire to use the language, and effort), beliefs and attitudes about oneself as a language learner, and anxiety (as related to public performance, language use with native speakers, making errors, comprehension, self-esteem, competition, tests, outcomes, and general comfort-discomfort with language learning). In addition, a negativity scale is available.

The entire instrument has a Cronbach alpha reliability index of .74 and a standardized item alpha of .82. Intrinsic motivation on the AFF is correlated with language proficiency (Ehrman and Oxford, 1995). Intrinsic motivation is also correlated with both speaking and reading proficiency, but more strongly with reading proficiency.

In the interest of time, the AFF was modified for use in the current study. We did not use the negativity scale, nor did we employ the sections on beliefs, attitudes, and anxiety. Thus, we chose to use only the most clearly "motivation-related" items in the survey. Of course, as other chapters in this book show, beliefs, attitudes, and anxiety all play a role in motivation, but we were seeking to measure the most straightforward aspects of motivation within a highly limited amount of time, even at the risk of somewhat lowered reliability.

The 28-item survey resulting from the modification contained 13 questions regarding intrinsic motivation, 5 for extrinsic motivation, 7 for desire to use the language outside of class, and 3 for effort.

DATA COLLECTION PROCEDURES

Questionnaires were sent to 150 students. Of the 150, 72 responded, providing a response rate of 48%. This was considered acceptable for an exploratory study such as the current one.

DATA ANALYSIS PROCEDURES

Pearson product moment correlation coefficients were computed between each strategy and each motivation item for learners of Japanese and Spanish separately. In addition to these, correlations between grades and strategy use were examined. An acceptable significance level was deemed to be $p<.05$.

T-tests, using the mean score of each element, were also computed to compare strategy use between learners of Spanish and Japanese. The Bonferroni correction was used to correct the test-wise error rate of $p<.05$ because more than one test was run; therefore, the experiment-wise error rate was $p<.005$, which we adopt here as the acceptable level of significance.

RESULTS

HYPOTHESIS 1:
Learners of Japanese are more motivated than learners of Spanish.

This hypothesis was supported. All the significant results of the t-tests showed that Japanese learners had higher motivation scores. The most remarkable of the differences are those related to intrinsic motivation. Of the 13 intrinsic motivation items, all were significant, showing that students of Japanese are more intrinsically motivated than students of Spanish. For example, these items were significant: "Studying the language is interesting," "I am glad to have the opportunity to learn the language," "The more I learn, the more I want to continue learning the language," "I want to learn as much of the language as I can," "I enjoy learning the language," "The satisfaction of language learning makes the effort worthwhile," "I want to learn many languages," "I make a point of trying to understand what I see and hear in the language," "I am glad to have the opportunity to learn the language," "I want to be fluent in the language," "The further along I go in my language studies, the more I want to keep studying the language," and "I plan to keep studying the language after completing this course." Thus, the students of Japanese won hands-down over the students of Spanish in intrinsic motivation.

Extrinsic motivation was assessed by five items but showed a significant ($p<.0027$) difference between students of Japanese and students of Spanish on only one item,

"Learning the language will enable me to better understand and appreciate the culture." Learners of Japanese were more extrinsically motivated, according to this item. Notice that this is an extrinsic motivation item, but it assesses interest in the culture, which relates to the integrative motivational orientation.

Of the seven items measuring the desire to use the language outside of class, six showed significance in favor of learners of Japanese. The significant items were: "I would use the language out of class," "If I had the opportunity, I would watch foreign language TV and listen to foreign language radio," "I would attend events involving the language or the culture," "I regularly use the language materials [outside of class]," "If available, I take advantage of opportunities to attend foreign language films, plays, or other cultural activities," and "I would read magazines, newspapers, or books in the language."

One of the three effort items, "I think about what I have learned in my language class during my spare time," reached significance, with learners of Japanese surpassing learners of Spanish.

In a nutshell, of the 28 items on the modified AFF, 19 (approximately 68%) reached significance, and all of these favored learners of Japanese over learners of Spanish.

HYPOTHESIS 2:
Learners of Japanese show more frequent use of
a wider range of strategies than do learners of Spanish.

This hypothesis was supported overall. Sixteen significant results were obtained from the SILL. These differences primarily showed that learners of Japanese were more frequent strategy users than learners of Spanish.

Among the 15 memory items in the abbreviated SILL, two demonstrated significant differences, one slanted toward Japanese learners ("I use a combination of sounds and images") and the other toward Spanish learners ("I use rhyming to remember a new word"). Thus, there was no great contrast between learners of Spanish and of Japanese in terms of their use of memory strategies.

For cognitive strategies, of which 18 were included in the questionnaire, only three showed significance. These were all in favor of learners of Japanese and included: "I look for patterns," "I develop my own understanding of how the language works," and "I imitate the talk of native speakers."

Of the seven compensation strategies, only one showed a significant difference, this time in the direction of the Spanish students: "I use gestures or switch back to my own language momentarily if I cannot think of the right expression."

Metacognitive strategies, those strategies which are aimed at improved management of one's own learning through planning and evaluating, exhibited the most contrast between students of Japanese and Spanish. The significant differences were all to the advantage of Japanese learners: "I arrange my schedule for language learning consistently," "I find opportunities to practice the language," and "I try to notice errors and find out the reasons for them," "I preview the lesson to get a general idea," and "I look for people with whom to speak the language." However, another significant difference was directed toward the Spanish learners: "I organize my language notebook to record important information."

No significant differences occurred among the seven affective strategies. Among the eight social strategies, just one was significant, "I pay close attention to the thoughts and feelings of others with whom I interact in the language," in favor of students of Japanese.

In short, of the 13 significant or significant differences in strategy use noted above, all except three (i.e., 77%) were to the advantage of learners of Japanese. This means that Japanese students were more frequent users of strategies of various kinds, especially metacognitive strategies for self-management and cognitive strategies for processing new information.

It is also important to look at the average frequencies, as shown in Table 2. For the most part, learners of Japanese tended to use the strategies named above at a moderate to frequent rate (M=3.0 to 4.3), except for rhyming and organizing a notebook (both low, 1.9 and 2.7). Learners of Spanish did not use rhyming very often (2.8), but significantly more frequently than learners of Japanese. Learners of Spanish employed the metacognitive strategies infrequently except for notebook organizing (3.6) and noticing errors (3.1). Use of gestures or code-switching was a popular strategy (4.2) among students of Spanish.

In metacognition, where Japanese students reigned supreme, there was at least a one-point difference (out of five) between the two language groups on all the significant contrasts. Such striking comparisons were only observed for metacognitive strategies.

HYPOTHESIS 3:
Significant correlations exist between
motivation and strategy use for each language group.

Correlation coefficients for total strategy use and total motivation were significant in both languages: r=.56 for Japanese (p<.002) and r=.58 for Spanish (p<.0003). Significant correlations were also found for numerous other combinations. Tables 1 and 2 show the significant correlations common to both groups and then unique to one group or the other.

Table 1: Significant correlations in both language groups

Correlations between...	Japanese Group		Spanish Group	
	r	p	r	p
Metacognitive strategies and effort	.74	.0001	.63	.0001
Metacognitive strategies and total motivation	.72	.0001	.69	.0001
Total strategy use and desire to use the L2	.72	.0001	.40	.0181
Metacognitive strategies and desire to use the L2	.69	.0001	.50	.0024
Social strategies and extrinsic motivation	.64	.0001	.34	.0433
Metacognitive strategies and intrinsic motivation	.57	.0014	.62	.0001
Cognitive strategies and intrinsic motivation	.61	.0005	.58	.0003
Social strategies and desire to use the L2	.59	.0005	.38	.0254
Total strategy use and effort	.55	.0017	.57	.0003
Social strategies and total motivation	.43	.0169	.53	.0011
Total strategy use and intrinsic motivation	.37	.0487	.51	.0016
Cognitive strategies and total motivation	.46	.0110	.34	.0430
Cognitive strategies and effort	.36	.0495	.34	.0447

Table 2: Significant correlations in the Japanese group only or the Spanish group only

Correlations between...	Japanese Group		Spanish Group	
	r	p	r	p
Cognitive strategies and desire to use the L2	.58	.0007		
Metacognitive strategies and extrinsic motivation	.47	.0092		
Total strategy use and extrinsic motivation	.46	.0100		
Compensation strategies and extrinsic motivation	.41	.0250		

Memory strategies and intrinsic motivation	.58	.0003		
Memory strategies and total motivation	.57	.0004		
Memory strategies and effort			.54	.0009
Social strategies and effort			.52	.0014
Social strategies and intrinsic motivation			.49	.0026
Affective strategies and total motivation			.47	.0046
Affective strategies and effort			.46	.0051
Memory strategies and desire to use the L2			.45	.0063
Affective strategies and desire to use the L2			.38	.0263
Affective strategies and intrinsic motivation			.37	.0298

In both language groups, total strategy use was significantly associated with intrinsic motivation, effort, and desire to use the language. This means that overall strategy use is directly tied to motivation (and vice versa).

Significant correlations in both language groups occurred for metacognitive strategy use on the one hand and effort, total motivation, desire to use the language outside of class, and intrinsic motivation on the other hand. For the Japanese group only, metacognitive strategy use correlated significantly with extrinsic motivation.

Within each group, cognitive strategy use was significantly linked with intrinsic motivation, total motivation, and effort. For the students of Japanese, cognitive strategy use was significantly associated with desire to use the language.

Social strategy use showed a significant association with extrinsic motivation, desire to use the language, and total motivation for both language groups. In the Spanish group, social strategy use was connected to effort and intrinsic motivation.

The use of affective strategies was related to desire to use the language, intrinsic motivation, effort, and total motivation within the Spanish group only. There were no significant connections between affective strategy use and any motivational element for learners of Japanese.

Memory strategy use showed an association with intrinsic motivation, effort, desire to use the language, and total motivation, but only for the Spanish group. Memory strategy use did not relate to motivation for Japanese students.

Compensation strategy use was related only to extrinsic motivation, and this occurred just for Japanese learners, not for Spanish learners.

DISCUSSION AND INTERPRETATION OF RESULTS

MOTIVATION BY LANGUAGE GROUP

Learners of Japanese scored significantly higher on motivation items than learners of Spanish in all of the categories: intrinsic motivation, extrinsic motivation, desire to use the language outside of class, and effort, thus indicating a stronger desire to learn the language. Learners of Japanese showed a strong interest in language learning in general and were willing to make a strong effort because of the satisfaction they found in learning Japanese. They were more interested in the target culture as well as the language and were more likely to seek opportunities to partake of extracurricular language activities such as watching TV, reading newspapers, and talking to native speakers. Generally speaking, their urge to study the language was rather integrative, indicating their willingness to know the target culture and people through language learning.

Obviously learners of Japanese must be motivated enough to choose this difficult Level IV language. Such a language for English speakers requires strenuous effort to achieve fluency. Therefore, a language this difficult would normally be shunned by students who choose to learn a language merely to meet a language requirement or earn additional A's on their report cards.

Significantly lower levels of motivation among learners of Spanish may partly be attributed to the fact that Spanish is easier for English speakers and is thus more likely to be chosen for the purpose of meeting a language requirement. The structural and lexical similarities, familiarity with the writing system, and cultural closeness all serve as possible reasons for the choice of Spanish by at least some students who seek "easy" profit with less effort. Certainly not all learners of Spanish fit this profile, but college language program administrators throughout the US would vouch for the existence of many such students.

STRATEGY USE BY LANGUAGE GROUP

The study also showed that students of Japanese reported using a significantly greater use of strategies than students of Spanish. Our assumption was that the more motivated the learner is, the more he or she is likely to use a range of learning strategies at a high frequency level. Learners of Japanese, who were more motivated than learners of Spanish, clearly overshadowed Spanish students in the frequency of strategy use in cognitive, metacognitive, social, and affective categories.

Only for certain strategies (not for a whole strategy category) did the learners of Spanish surpass learners of Japanese: rhyming for memorization, code-switching or gestures, and learning through comparison with the native language. Learners of Japanese could not use these three strategies very often. Rhyming, code-switching, and cross-language comparisons are difficult for learners of Japanese because their native language is so different from the target language. Gestures might be less useful for Japanese learners than for Spanish learners because of cultural issues associated with gesturing.

Most conspicuous was the high frequency of use of metacognitive strategies among learners of Japanese. These students scored higher than their Spanish-learning counterparts regarding use of a large array of metacognitive strategies, such as previewing the lesson, arranging their schedules for learning, finding opportunities to practice, finding opportunities to speak with native speakers, and learning through errors. This strikingly higher rate of metacognitive strategy use among learners of Japanese may be interpreted in terms of the approach used in their classroom. As mentioned earlier, most of the learners of Japanese in this study are taught by instructors who were trained under Dr. Eleanor Jorden, who emphasizes memorization of core conversation, practicing at home with audiotapes, gaining accuracy in pronunciation and structure, and taking increased responsibility for one's own learning. It is therefore assumed that learners of Japanese are strongly encouraged by the nature of the course to become more organized (previewing, scheduling, practicing). The great emphasis on oral-aural work fosters the desire to find native speakers with whom to talk. The stress on accuracy clearly relates to the strategy of learning through errors.

Relatively lower metacognitive strategy performance among learners of Spanish can be partially explained by the classroom approach. Unlike learners of Japanese who are accustomed to memorizing core conversations or substitution drills that reflect an emphasis on structural accuracy, learners of Spanish practice the language through an approach that allows learners to interact freely with less focus on precision. Accordingly, the focus is on classroom interaction rather than on practice at home with tapes or scheduled preparation for class (no matter what the textbook authors or teachers might intend).

However, the special nature of learners of Japanese — highly motivated and typically academically strong — suggests that other factors besides the classroom approach are at play in terms of their frequent metacognitive strategy use. Likewise, the less motivated learners of Spanish tended to use metacognitive strategies less frequently, so classroom approach is not the only factor that seems important in metacognitive strategy use. It must be remembered that the use of metacognitive strategies was highly related to multiple aspects of motivation.

Learners of Japanese proved to use certain affective and social strategies more often than learners of Spanish to facilitate their learning process. They were more likely to be aware of and control their attitudes and feelings, to be more attentive to the thoughts and feelings of the person with whom they interact, and to encourage themselves to be more involved with the target language and culture. More frequent use of affective and social strategies among Japanese learners may be partly due to the unfamiliarity with the language that requires emotional control and a positive attitude on the part of the learner. It also stands to reason that learners of Japanese, who are more motivated, enthusiastic, and confident of their ability, may well use strategies that help maintain high self-esteem.

MOTIVATION BY TOTAL STRATEGY USE AND BY STRATEGY CATEGORY

As noted above, both language groups showed that total strategy use was significantly associated with intrinsic motivation, effort, and desire to use the language. No causality can be inferred from these results. However, let us speculate about possibilities. It might be that motivation spurs strategy use. Alternatively, it might be that strategy use leads to better language performance, which in itself is likely to be motivating and might thus lead to increased strategy use in a spiraling or cycling mode.

It is important to recognize the very strong relationships between metacognitive strategy use and several motivational aspects in both language groups. Metacognition, which in much research tends to distinguish successful from less successful learners (Oxford, 1993), is closely tied to motivation. Learners with a strong will to pursue their goals would no doubt be active in planning, organizing, and evaluating their own study.

Similarly, cognitive and social strategy use was associated with several motivational elements in both groups. This means that in both groups, the more motivated the learner, the greater the employment of cognitive and social strategies.

However, use of affective and memory strategies was related to motivation only in the Spanish group. The more motivated the Spanish learners were, the more they tended to use affective and memory strategies. This particular pattern did not occur for Japanese learners, who were highly motivated overall.

Compensation strategies had little relationship to motivation, and that association was only for extrinsic motivation among learners of Japanese. In this study, compensation strategies did not play a major role.

CLASSROOM IMPLICATIONS

This study demonstrates that learners who are more motivated tend to use a wider range of strategies more frequently. This suggests that learning strategies are an important element in the learning process and that teachers and students might benefit from an explicit discussion of strategies. Research shows that strategies can be improved through overt explanation and practice and that strategy improvement contributes to better performance (O'Malley and Chamot, 1990). It can be hypothesized that improvement of strategies can be highly motivating, particularly if students realize that it is their strategic effort that creates greater language skill.

To maximize language learning in the classroom, it is desirable to employ activities that engage and enhance the learners' motivation. Because this investigation shows that learners are interested in culture as well as language, motivation might be stimulated by weaving culture into language classes more effectively. Culture can be used as the content of conversations, tapes, and readings. Introduction of sociolinguistic aspects, which are closely related to culture, can improve communicative competence while simultaneously enhancing motivation. Cultural elements in games, simulations, and role-plays can motivate learners and also reduce anxiety.

In this study, we found that learners use different strategies to learn different languages. The use of particular strategies or sets of strategies seems tied in a complex way to levels of motivation, kinds of motivation, nature of the language being learned, amount of cultural and linguistic stimulation available, and classroom instructional design. It is crucial to understand how these factors fit together. A major model of language learning needs to be developed that includes these factors. In most of the previous models, the nature of the target language — which is so important in the current study — has unfortunately been omitted.

Of course, the variables just listed do not include additional factors that might influence language learning and language performance: characteristics of the teacher, learning styles of the students, general and state-specific anxiety, and a host of beliefs and attitudes that were not assessed in this study. As seen in Chapters 4 and 6 in this volume, anxiety, beliefs, and attitudes are related to motivation. All of these would need to be included in a comprehensive theory of language learning or a truly explanatory model of language learning motivation.

Rebecca L. Oxford & Jill Shearin
The University of Alabama

CHAPTER 6
LANGUAGE LEARNING MOTIVATION
IN A NEW KEY

ABSTRACT

As an area of research and practice, language learning motivation has been dominated by social psychology for the last thirty years. For that duration social psychology was the home of the *only* theory that explained why and how students chose to learn languages. That theory was extraordinarily helpful and spawned dozens of books, research articles, dissertations, and theses. No matter how useful, the theory failed to include some factors that might be considered by some experts to be essential to language learning motivation. As demonstrated by this chapter, researchers outside of social psychology have started to speak up, at long last investigating additional concepts of motivation in the lives of second and foreign language learners. These investigators are not iconoclasts; they do not want to destroy the social psychology framework that has been so carefully built. They want, nevertheless, to expand that framework by considering important ideas offered not just by social psychology, but also by other branches of psychology: general, industrial, educational, cognitive developmental, and sociocultural psychology, for example. This chapter portrays some of the rich ferment taking place now in the area of language learning motivation.

INTRODUCTION

Is motivation important to second or foreign language (L2) learning? What does motivation contribute to L2 success, over and above that which is contributed by a talent or aptitude for learning languages? The answer is that motivation is one of the main determining factors in success in developing a second or foreign language (Gardner, 1985b; Scarcella and Oxford, 1992). Motivation determines the extent of active, personal involvement in foreign or second language learning. Conversely, unmotivated students are insufficiently involved and therefore unable to develop their potential L2 skills.

Motivation is important because it directly influences how often students use L2 learning strategies, how much students interact with native speakers, how much input they receive in the language being learned (the target language), how well they do on curriculum-related achievement tests, how high their general proficiency level becomes, and how long they persevere and maintain L2 skills after language study is over (Ely, 1986a, 1986b; Gardner, 1992; Scarcella and Oxford, 1992).

Oxford, Rebecca & Shearin, Jill (1996). Language learning motivation in a new key. In Rebecca Oxford (Ed.), *Language Learning Motivation: Pathways to the New Century.* (Technical Report #11) (pp. 121–144). Honolulu: University of Hawai'i, Second Language Teaching & Curriculum Center.

Therefore, motivation is crucial for L2 learning, and it is essential to understand what our students' motivations are. Nevertheless, the prevalent theory of language learning motivation in the last three decades has not adequately explained all the reasons for language learning and all the personal, "individual-difference" factors that come into play. Chapter 1 describes that theory in brief terms and shows how the theory has started to evolve in new ways very recently.

This chapter goes beyond the existing L2 theory of motivation, which comes almost exclusively from social psychology, and calls for an expansion that includes many other branches of psychology: general, industrial, educational, cognitive developmental, and sociocultural psychology. In this push for growth, we do not want to lose the social psychological concepts that helped us so much. Indeed, we are standing on the shoulders of giants, such as Robert Gardner and his research colleagues, who have given us our earliest views of language learning motivation. We hope this chapter ultimately enhances the increasing unity within this research area and that it helps more theorists, teachers, and students benefit from L2 learning motivation research.

This chapter suggests ways by which the notion of L2 learning motivation might be expanded. We want to maintain the best of the existing L2 learning motivation theory and push its parameters outward. Therefore, we offer motivation material that is well known in many areas of psychology but that has not yet been directly applied to motivation in the L2 field. This chapter, like the others in this book, will stimulate much more interaction on the topic throughout the L2 field, with the result being the eventual development of a more comprehensive model of L2 learning motivation.

The chapter is organized as follows:

1. Necessity of expanding the prevalent theory of L2 learning motivation

2. Exploration of useful theories from other avenues of psychology

3. Summary of key instructional implications

4. Recommendations for research

NECESSITY OF EXPANDING THE PREVALENT L2 LEARNING MOTIVATION THEORY

The best known theory of L2 learning motivation, a theory based on social psychology, does not cover all the possible reasons for learning a new language. Let us consider an example (Oxford, 1992). At the beginning of the fall term, 218 American high school students were asked to write an essay explaining their reasons for studying Japanese. Many wanted to learn Japanese for future business reasons (an instrumental orientation), and others were spurred by the desire to make friends in Japan (an integrative orientation). However, more than two-thirds of the teenagers also had additional reasons for learning Japanese that did not relate well to either of these two orientations. These reasons included: receiving intellectual stimulation, seeking personal challenge, enjoying the elitism of taking a difficult language, showing off to friends, developing greater cultural tolerance through language study, aiding world peace, satisfying curiosity about cultural "secrets," pursuing a fascination with Japanese writing systems, and having a private code that parents would not know. These were only a sampling of the reasons students stated for studying Japanese. Most students spontaneously listed and explained at least three or four reasons per person, reasons that when analyzed resulted in approximately twenty distinguishable categories. In addition, they said they thought that learning Japanese would make them more self-confident, although that was not the reason they were choosing the language.

Furthermore, the prevalent theory of L2 learning motivation does not often discuss developmental changes in a particular student's motivation, although changes in interests and anxiety levels (see, e.g., Gardner and MacIntyre, 1993) can influence motivational changes. Here are two stories in which L2 learning motivation changed drastically over time. In one illustration, the author was a teenager who learned the Cyrillic alphabet so she and her boyfriend could have a secret code to use while passing notes in church. The next year she signed up for Russian in college because it was challenging and had prestige value. Later she majored in Russian for instrumental career reasons and then taught Russian briefly in two settings, a high school and a university. After being away from Russian for a long while, she saw the language as a valuable communication tool and renewed her Russian skills through individualized telephone tutoring. Curry (1990) provides the second illustration. Her son started out taking a Japanese language course simply to fulfill a college language requirement, later became intellectually entranced with the language and culture, and still later wanted to live and work in Japan and use the language every day. In these two examples of motivational development, effortful behavior can be considered a motivational spark rather than just a result of motivation. In these examples, initial participation led to increased interest, which then led to further involvement and to developmental changes in the reasons for L2 learning. Until recently, no theory of L2 learning motivation paid much attention to such developmental changes.

THEORY EXPANSION THROUGH EXPLORATION OF OTHER AVENUES OF PSYCHOLOGY

In this section we explore several additional theories that might help enlarge the existing concept of L2 learning motivation in a helpful fashion. Specifically, we discuss four broad classes of motivation theories from general psychology: need theories, instrumentality theories, equity theories, and reinforcement theories. We also see how industrial psychologists have integrated some of these theories with social cognition concepts to produce an enlarged motivation theory. We consider how educational psychologists have applied some of these ideas to classroom learning. Finally, we investigate theories of Piaget (cognitive developmental psychology) and Vygotsky (sociocultural psychology) as possible sources of explanation for L2 learning motivation. Because each of the elements has very practical instructional implications for the L2 classroom, we share our suggestions as we go along, as well as providing a synthesis of some key implications in the final section.

NEED THEORIES

Landy (1985) notes two significant types of need theories: (1) hierarchies of need and (2) need-achievement. These are based on a need that creates tension until satisfied. Showing a new side to their thinking, Gardner and Tremblay (1994a, 1994b) now praise the budding influence of need theories on L2 learning motivation theory.

Hierarchies of need

The best known need hierarchy is by Maslow (1970). According to Maslow, individuals instigate, direct, and sustain activity to satisfy certain needs that are hierarchical in nature, beginning with biological needs and progressing upward to psychological ones. Maslow's hierarchy of needs progresses as follows: (1) physiological, (2) safety and security, (3) belongingness and love, (4) esteem, and (5) self-actualization. Alderfer (1969, 1972) and Herzberg (1966) produced need hierarchies similar to those of Maslow. Alderfer showed how people regress if their higher-order needs are not met. Research on Maslow's need hierarchy has raised a number of questions and contradictions (Hall and Nougain, 1968; Lawler and Suttle, 1972; Rauschenberger, Schmitt, and Hunter, 1980; Wahba and Bridwell, 1976). However, the basic concept is intuitively attractive: that fundamental physical needs must be met before more psychological needs can be satisfied.

Implications of hierarchies of need

Assuming that Maslow's hierarchy has some truth, we can see that foreign and second language learners might have somewhat different motivations related to their varying needs. In the foreign language setting, needs do not relate to physiology or physical safety, although they often relate to emotional or psychological security. Non-physical safety and security needs may show up in the foreign language classroom, where risk-taking cannot occur unless students feel psychologically secure (see Brown, 1987; Horwitz, 1990; Horwitz and Young, 1991; Moskowitz, 1972; Scarcella and Oxford, 1992; Stevick, 1995). Needs (and thus motivation) for foreign language learners would center on the psychological aspects of the second rung in the hierarchy and, when those needs are satisfied, would relate to the third, fourth, and fifth rungs in the hierarchy. Motivation would be differently focused for second language learners, whose needs would be negotiated in the target language from the very lowest levels of the hierarchy; even physiological, physical safety, and physical security needs might not be assured without the use of the target language. L2 learners can regress in their needs, motivation, and performance if their requirements for psychological security are not met.

Insecure L2 learners can be very anxious (for background see Horwitz and Young, 1991; MacIntyre and Gardner, 1989, 1991a, 1991b). Teachers can reduce this anxiety and foster greater psychological security by noticing signs of anxiety, developing a nonthreatening classroom climate, helping students relax through music and laughter, using emotional checklists for student self-awareness, showing students how to use self-encouragement techniques, avoiding sarcasm and sharp criticism, using praise well, and developing peer support networks (Horwitz, 1990; Horwitz and Young, 1991; Moskowitz, 1972; Oxford, 1990a, 1990c; Scarcella and Oxford, 1992).

Job satisfaction

Need hierarchies are closely related to job satisfaction, and job satisfaction research is directly relevant to L2 learning satisfaction. Herzberg suggested that jobs can be enriched to provide greater intrinsic satisfaction. Following Herzberg (1966), the workplace researchers Hackman and Oldham (1975, 1976) provided a job enrichment model showing that the actual responsibilities of a job are capable of motivating certain individuals who have a high need for growth. In order to have motivation potential for such people, a job must have these qualities: (1) skill variety, (2) clear and significant tasks, (3) autonomy for the worker, and (4) feedback for the worker.

Implications of job satisfaction

Internally directed L2 learners who have high needs for growth will be motivated to learn the target language as long as the process of learning involves these enrichment qualities: variety, tasks that are identified and important, self-direction, and frequent and appropriate feedback. Externally directed L2 learners also respond well to variety, clear and significant tasks, and useful feedback, although they often need more specific guidance from the teacher than do internally directed learners. The L2 teacher has a clear role in providing a learning situation with these characteristics. Specific illustrations of how this can be done are found in recent books (Cohen, 1990; Oxford, 1990a, 1990c; Scarcella and Oxford, 1992).

Need-achievement, fear of failure, and fear of success

The second need theory of motivation is based on the need for achievement (usually known as need-achievement) and the related "fear of failure" and "fear of success" tendencies. The early work of Murray (1938) and McClelland (1955) suggested that certain environmental cues motivate people because these cues are associated with some past success or failure. Past success in a particular situation would make a person more likely to engage in achievement behaviors in a similar situation in the future; past failure would generate fear and stifle achievement behavior. Most need theorists agree that the kinds of situations that characteristically evoke need-achievement are those in which competence of performance is the focus (Crandall, 1963).

Need-achievement was once viewed as a relatively stable, generalized personality trait to strive for success in a situation in which standards of success are applicable (McClelland, 1955). However, the Crandall group (Crandall, 1963; Crandall and Battle, 1970; Crandall, Dewey, Katovsky, and Preston, 1960) noted that need-achievement is not global, applying to all situations, but instead varies markedly from one achievement area to another for a given person. Research by Steers and Porter (1975) demonstrated a correlation between performance and satisfaction for individuals with a high need for achievement, but not for those whose need to achieve is low. Although good performance is, by itself, a reward for those who need to achieve, even better performance can be created by making their tasks more challenging and autonomous. Veroff (1969), foreshadowing the self-efficacy and attribution theories of social cognition (discussed later in this article), distinguished between autonomous achievement motivation and social comparison achievement motivation, with categories based on an interaction between two factors: (1) whether the individual emphasizes the process of having achieved or the impact of the accomplishment; and (2) whether the person derives standards of excellence from inside himself or herself, from some social reference, or from an impersonal task demand. Stein and Bailey (1973) suggested that need-achievement is stimulated by social factors (external factors for many females and internal factors for many males). The controversial concept of "fear of success" (Horner, 1968, 1970) was found to apply more often to white females than white males because of the formers' desire to please those around them and the desire to avoid loss of social support (affiliation) through too great a success. Blacks showed a reversal, with fear of success occurring significantly more often in males than in females. These results were related to sex-role expectations in various ethnic groups.

Implications of need-achievement, fear of failure, and fear of success

Need-achievement theory relates directly to an expanded concept of L2 learning motivation. Many L2 students feel the need to achieve, some feel the need to avoid failure, and a few might even experience the need to avoid success (even if they desire success to some degree). Need-achievement theory implies that L2 teachers must provide students with work that leads to success, and students must believe that doing the specified tasks will produce positive results and that these results are personally valuable. Past success encourages greater effort in the future by heightening the need for achievement, as long as the value of success is perceived as strong. L2 teachers must be aware that the factors that stimulate the need for achievement might differ from one student to another. They must find out which aspects of L2 learning are personally valuable to students and must design tasks that support those aspects. For example, if students highly value the skill of speaking, classroom activities must encourage development of this skill and must have positive results. This means that activities must be designed and paced appropriately for the individuals involved. Although this assertion seems like common sense, the converse can be seen in the uncompromising, lock-step, text-and-syllabus-driven approach used by many university L2 programs and by the preference of some educators to limit the first two years of foreign language study to only certain language skills. Because L2 learning can be a highly social process, females are often keenly stimulated to achieve in this area, and one striking feature of the L2 teaching field (as shown in the attendance rolls of any major professional conference and in employment figures) is the preponderance of women, at least at particular educational levels. Fear of success can occur when and if achievement in the L2 learning field is likely to cause loss of affiliation; but this is typically not the case for L2 learners (except in the most academically competitive foreign language environments). Fear of failure (see especially Horner, 1970) is more salient for most L2 learners than fear of success. Even the best L2 learners have experienced failures in communication. Teachers need to make learners feel comfortable even when communication is not perfect.

INSTRUMENTALITY (EXPECTANCY-VALUE) THEORIES

A second broad class of motivation theories includes instrumentality theories, which suggest that individuals engage in activities instrumental in achieving some valued outcome. Instrumentality theories are more elaborated and generalized than any concept of instrumental motivation mentioned earlier. Instrumentality theories emphasize cognition and the process by which an individual answers the question, "Should I expend the energy or not?" Unlike the tension-creating need theories, instrumentality theories focus on the individual's expectation of receiving a valued reward. This is why they are sometimes called "expectancy-value" theories. Also unlike need theories, which are sometimes very specific about their hierarchical nature and the ways to satisfy identified needs, instrumentality theories are rather vague about the nature of these rewards.

Atkinson's expectancy-value theory

Atkinson (1964) asserted that engagement in achievement-oriented behaviors is a function not only of the motivation for success, but also the probability of success (expectancy) and the incentive value (sometimes called valence) of success. The flip side of this success-satisfaction coin, however, is the failure-shame side. Given a previous failure experience in which one was ridiculed or punished, there is subsequently a tendency to avoid failure by choosing a task so easy that one cannot fail, or one so hard that there is no shame in failure.

VIE theory

Early instrumentality theories, such as the path-goal theory (Georgopolis, Mahoney, and Jones, 1951), were later formalized in the VIE (valence, instrumentality, expectancy) theory (Vroom, 1964). According to the VIE theory, individuals ask themselves: (1) Does the outcome, e.g., a good grade, have value (valence)? (2) Will the outcome yield other positive results (instrumentality), such as a useful skill, job advancement, or graduation? (3) Are my actions likely to lead to success (expectancy)?

Goal-setting theory

To explain motivated behavior, instrumentality theory is often combined with goal-setting theory, which proposes that performance is closely related to an individual's accepted goals. After reviewing fifteen years of goal-setting research, Locke, Shaw, Saari, and Latham (1981) concluded that: (1) goal-setting and performance are related; (2) goals affect task performance by focusing attention and action, mobilizing energy, prolonging persistence, and motivating the development of relevant strategies for goal attainment; (3) difficult, specific goals produce higher performance levels than no goals, easy goals, or vague, "do your best" goals; (4) before goal-setting will affect an individual's performance, she or he must have the prerequisite ability for high performance; (5) feedback is also necessary for high performance; (6) concrete rewards such as money may increase commitment to an accepted goal; (7) assigned goals, if accepted by the individual, have the same effect as goals that the individual sets; (8) ability is the only individual difference variable that has had an effect on goal-setting behavior; i.e., need-achievement and self-esteem have not significantly influenced goal-setting behavior.

Note that several motivation experts have integrated the two instrumentalist theories of VIE and goal-setting (Mento, Cartledge, and Locke, 1980; Matsui, Okada, and Mizuguchi, 1981; Jahoda, 1981).

Based on our own research, we know that individual differences in learning style — not just in ability — directly affect goal-setting behavior (Oxford, Ehrman, and Lavine, 1991). Extroverted, feeling-oriented students are likely to opt for goals that involve communication with other people, while introverted, thinking-oriented students are slanted toward goals that involve heavy analysis and individual work. Closure-focused people want set, detailed goals that they know they can reach in a given period of time, while more open individuals want vaguer goals that are not well fixed and that can be readily changed as the situation warrants. These learning style differences, based on personal values, are reflected not only in the selection of goals but also in the behaviors used to achieve those goals. (For details, see Oxford, Ehrman, and Lavine, 1991; Reid, 1995.)

Implications of instrumentality (expectancy-value) theory

Expectancy-value theory helps remind us that L2 learners' expectancies of success or failure are very important in determining their motivation to learn the language. Other important factors include L2 learners' beliefs about whether their learning performance will lead to something else (career enhancement, general enjoyment, greater cultural tolerance) and whether these outcomes are meaningful and valuable. If language learners do not believe that their performance leads anywhere or is ultimately valuable, their motivation will be lowered. Goals should be specific, hard but achievable, accepted by the students, and accompanied by feedback about progress. The goal-setting process is directly influenced by learning styles of the people involved, and the subsequent goal-attainment behavior is also a reflection of style preferences. Learners' goals, along with feedback from the L2 teacher and any other relevant sources, help determine expenditure of energy (motivated behavior) the students will put forth. Goal-setting can have exceptional importance in stimulating L2 learning motivation, and it is therefore rather shocking that so little time and energy are spent in the L2 classroom on goal-setting.

EQUITY THEORIES

A third group of motivation theories concerns equity (Pritchard, 1969), which is characterized by a mathematical ratio of inputs to outcomes (Adams, 1965, 1975). Inputs include intellectual ability, personality traits, experience, psychomotor skills, seniority — anything the individual believes he or she contributes to the work setting. Outcomes include grades, performance ratings, money, promotions, praise — anything that results from the situation that the individual perceives as having personal value. Once individuals have set up this ratio, they compare the value of that ratio to their own internal standards or to the value of the ratio for significant others. If a person perceives a discrepancy, unhappiness and demotivation result (Landy, 1985).

Implications of equity theories

Equity theories are related to L2 learning motivation because the learner must believe that the probable results are worth the effort expended. If the learner feels that many years of arduous L2 learning are likely to produce very slender outcomes (in terms of proficiency, enjoyment, social interaction, or language utility on the job), the learner will become less motivated to continue. This happens frequently, as witnessed by the high drop-out rate as soon as official language requirements are met and as shown by comments like, "Learning French isn't worth the energy; I can't even order a cup of coffee or glass of wine in French after two years of studying!" In many L2 programs students learn about the L2 rather than learning to use it. Foreign language students on graduating from high school after several years of language study typically have reached only the 0+ proficiency level (novice high), at which they can barely communicate at all; foreign language majors in college usually top out at 2+ (advanced-plus), where they can only talk about concrete subjects and still make many errors (Omaggio Hadley, 1993). To many students, these outcomes often do not seem to be worth the price, and motivation therefore plummets.

On the other hand, if all the effort is viewed as leading to significant outcomes, that is, if the ratio is deemed positive, then the language learner will feel continuously motivated. For students to be motivated, they need repeated evidence — often from teachers but also from successful users of the target language who were once in the students' own place — that the benefits of L2 learning outweigh the costs. It is important for L2 teachers to know what students' goals are so that they can provide the type of instruction that leads to the expected outcome, e.g., provide more communicative classroom activities if the goal is communicative survival skills like ordering in a restaurant, making purchases, or using the transportation system.

REINFORCEMENT THEORIES

Reinforcement highlights the fourth set of motivation theories. This set attributes individual behavior to the stimulus-response-reward association. Rewards may be contingent or noncontingent, intrinsic or extrinsic. Contingent rewards, those that occur only if certain behaviors happen, yield higher levels of effort and production than noncontingent rewards, like weekly or monthly pay. Behaviorists contend that contingent rewards yield higher levels of effort and production than noncontingent rewards. By extension, then, energy expenditure (motivated behavior) results from response-reward contingencies.

Much interest and research have been devoted to this issue of rewards and how they relate to motivation. Critics have taken exception on two fronts, conceptual and empirical. On the conceptual front, Scott (1976) raised the question of whether the terms "intrinsic" and "extrinsic" belong to the task or the individual. The inability of psychologists to agree on which of a series of rewards are intrinsic or extrinsic exacerbates the confusion surrounding research (Dyer and Parker, 1975).

On the empirical front, the basic findings of some researchers (Arnold, 1976; Deci, 1972; Lepper and Greene, 1975; Scott, 1976; Scott and Erskine, 1980) have not been replicated in subsequent studies. The only safe conclusion that can be drawn at this point is that rewards interact in a complex manner with task characteristics. "More [reward] is not always better" (Landy, p. 371). Among others, Locke (1980) has noted the limitations of behaviorism in understanding work behavior and has suggested that the cognitive interpretation as a broader, more complex approach is appropriate.

Implications of reinforcement theories

Reinforcement theories are often the most widely used motivation theories in the L2 classroom. In fact, these theories are usually the only ones with which L2 teachers are acquainted, although other motivation theories are probably more useful. Gardner and Tremblay (1994a) note that one of the greatest movements in motivation theory has been the advent of the concept that learning could exist without external rewards. However, language teachers consistently reward students through praise and through a variety of grades (on tests, classroom assignments, homework assignments, and report cards or term grading sheets). Sometimes teachers give tangible prizes as rewards. However, intrinsic rewards — those that come from inside the student or from the language task itself — are often more powerful than teacher-provided rewards. Teachers can help students see the intrinsic rewards of L2 learning as well as providing the extrinsic rewards many students want.

EXPANDING THESE CONCEPTS AND ADDING SOCIAL COGNITION

Industrial psychologists Locke and Latham (1990) have attempted to reconcile several of the motivation concepts above and have added social cognition theories (e.g., self-efficacy and attribution for success or failure) to leaven the mix. Their work has implications for L2 learning motivation. These researchers describe two work stages, the motivation-performance stage and the rewards-satisfaction stage.

Motivation-performance stage

In this stage, Locke and Latham (1990) explain the motivation to work by integrating goal-setting theory and expectancy-value theory with yet another theory so far not discussed here: self-efficacy. In order for goals to affect performance, there must be (1) commitment to the goals even if assigned by others, (2) feedback on performance in relation to one's goals, (3) ability of the individual to reach or approach the goals, and (4) role modeling and sometimes tangible incentives. Without goals, feedback is meaningless, and without feedback, the person doesn't have a clear assessment of progress toward goals. Expectancy-value theory is woven into the explanation of motivation to perform with Vroom's (1964) proposal that expectancy (effort will lead to successful performance) is positively associated with performance level when instrumentality (performance will lead to rewards) and valence (the perceived value of the outcomes of performance) are held constant.

The concept of self-efficacy, a broadened view of expectancy, is drawn from social cognition theory and plays an important role in explaining motivation to achieve. Self-efficacy is one's judgment of how well one can execute courses of action required to deal with a certain kind of task. "Self-esteem may be the aggregation of self-efficacy perceptions across a broad range of specific tasks," say Gist, Schwoerer, and Rosen, (1989, p. 884).

Self-efficacy involves the concept that performance will lead to rewards and focuses on one's ability, creativity, adaptability, and capacity to perform in a particular situational context. Self-efficacy has been shown to affect performance positively and directly. High self-efficacy results in higher effort toward a goal, even in response to negative feedback (Bandura, 1982; Bandura and Cervone, 1986).

Bandura (1982) notes that high self-efficacy in learning is associated with heavy investment of cognitive effort and with superior learning performance, particularly in a situation that contains cognitive difficulty or uncertainty. High-goal individuals are more likely to believe that pursuing a goal results in achievement and skill improvement (Locke and Latham, 1990). Finally, higher goals produce higher standards for achieving self-satisfaction. High-standard individuals must accomplish more than low-standard individuals to believe they have performed successfully. Thus, high self-efficacy leads to higher goal striving and higher personal standards.

Bandura (1978, 1982) identifies four sources of information people use in assessing their self-efficacy: (1) past experiences of success or failure, (2) vicarious experiences of watching other students succeed or fail, (3) verbal persuasion or self-talk, and (4) physiological states such as exhaustion. Self-efficacy judgments affect task selection, level of effort, degree of persistence, and quality of performance

(Bandura, 1982). Individuals who have high self-efficacy tend to perform better than individuals low in self-efficacy. People avoid activities they expect exceed their capabilities, but they perform activities that they expect themselves capable of managing (Bandura and Schunk, 1981; Shunk, 1985). Thus, self-efficacy is based on expectancies.

Practically speaking, goals, expectancies, and self-efficacy affect performance because they: (1) lead individuals to persist longer at tasks; (2) lead individuals to exert more effort, especially on tasks with time limits; (3) direct attention toward goal-relevant action; (4) stimulate individuals to develop metacognitive plans for attaining goals; and (5) enhance the quality of analytic strategies used (Oxford and Shearin, 1994).

Implications of the motivation-performance stage

L2 learners with established goals and a sense of self-efficacy will focus on learning tasks, persist at them, and develop strategies to complete tasks successfully so they can meet their goals. L2 learners must believe that they have some control over the outcomes because of their performance; they must feel a sense of effectiveness within themselves, so they will want to continue learning the target language. However, many L2 students do not have an initial belief in their own self-efficacy. They feel lost in the language class. L2 teachers can help such students develop a sense of self-efficacy by providing meaningful tasks at which students can succeed and over which students can have a feeling of control. Examples of relevant, clear-goaled, success-engendering language tasks (Celce-Murcia and Hilles, 1988; Cohen, 1990; Crookall and Oxford, 1990; Frank and Rinvolucri, 1983; Nunan, 1989a; Omaggio Hadley, 1993; Oxford, 1990a; Ur, 1984). Self-efficacy can also be developed by giving students a degree of choice in classroom activities from day to day (Oxford, 1990a). The L2 learning strategies students use are influenced by goals, expectancies, and self-efficacy. If L2 goals (set either by the teacher or the student) are unclear, if the student's expectancy of success is weak, and if the student's sense of self-efficacy is low, the student is unlikely to use higher-order thinking strategies or any other kind of useful learning strategies, because progress in learning the language just does not seem possible. Use of appropriate, well-orchestrated L2 learning strategies is extremely helpful to learning performance (Cohen, 1990; O'Malley and Chamot, 1990; Oxford, 1990a, 1990c; Wenden and Rubin, 1987). For this reason alone L2 teachers should work on improving goal-setting and positive self-talk by students.

Rewards-satisfaction stage

The relationship between motivation to achieve and satisfaction attained, according to Locke and Latham (1990), is revealed in the rewards-satisfaction stage. Self-administered rewards and self-satisfaction are important. Individuals compare their performance with internal goals or standards, which they have either set or accepted from others, and then self-administer rewards or punishments. Not unexpectedly, successful performance or progress leads to more satisfaction, pride in performance, and sense of achievement than does substandard performance. People usually credit themselves when successful but blame others when unsuccessful (Locke, 1976).

Attribution theory (Heider, 1958; Weiner, 1986) adds the concept that higher satisfaction occurs when success is self-attributed than when success is attributed to external factors. Attribution is the process by which people interpret the causes of events in their environment (Weiner, 1986). Attributions of causality are an attempt to impose order on what might otherwise be seen as chaotic experience. An underlying assumption is that one's attribution of causality influences one's behavior. Thus, knowing what someone thinks about causes might help explain how that person acts. People's attributions influence their expectancy of success, their emotional reactions to performance outcomes, their choice of tasks, and their persistence (Weiner, 1972, 1974).

Research has shown that the three major attributions are ability, effort, and luck (Weiner, 1979). Weiner (1979) proposes that these three attributions can be further analyzed along three dimensions: (1) locus of control (Rotter's 1966 concepts of external and internal locus), (2) stability (fixed or variable), and (3) controllability (controllable or uncontrollable). Accordingly, *ability* is classified as internal, stable, and uncontrollable. *Effort* is internal, unstable, and controllable. *Luck* is external, unstable, and uncontrollable — the worst possible combination from the point of view of self-efficacy. When people believe they — rather than luck, fate, the teacher, or an easy test — have created a successful performance, they are happier with themselves and their abilities. This positive relationship between goal success and satisfaction raises a dilemma: Whereas easy goals produce more satisfaction than difficult goals, difficult goals yield higher performance than easy goals. Locke and Latham (1990) offer a number of solutions to this dilemma, including moderating goals and defining goal difficulty in terms of time, thought, effort, and resources. Via their solutions, difficult goals would be achievable, yet still motivate high performance levels. Rewards and punishments (leading either toward or away from satisfaction) can also be administered by others. Equity theory argues that people evaluate their rewards and punishments in terms of fairness or equity by comparing outputs to inputs. If the person perceives inequitable rewards, he or she becomes dissatisfied and tries to restore equity by modifying performance or directly protesting. Thus, satisfaction is most likely to be achieved when an individual is successful in reaching goals and is rewarded fairly for high performance. Such action, in turn, leads to a higher level of commitment to the organization and its goals. The individual is much more likely to engage in citizenship behaviors like helping co-workers and doing extra work.

Implications of the rewards-satisfaction stage

Fair rewards and personal satisfaction are directly related to L2 learning. Rewards and satisfaction strengthen the learners' commitment to the L2 class and to the established goals and thus lead to continued motivation. L2 teachers can ensure that the rewards they give are fair and can stimulate students to seek personal satisfaction in their learning. Students' satisfaction can also be associated with self-reward, a long-neglected area of research in L2 learning. Self-reward is discussed elsewhere (Oxford, 1990a) along with the necessary, concomitant accurate self-evaluation that precedes self-reward. L2 teachers can also apply reward-satisfaction theory by providing instructional activities, exercises, and tests in which students will be challenged, yet successful, so that they attribute their success to their own effort and hard work. L2 researchers Gardner and Tremblay (1994a) rightly hail the application of locus of control concepts to language learning.

MASTERY MODEL OF EDUCATIONAL ACHIEVEMENT

So far we have described various motivation theories and have made our own creative applications to language learning situations. Educational psychologists Ames and Archer (1988) have extended several motivation theories into classrooms in general. Ames and Archer have examined the relationship between motivation and goal-setting in the classroom, particularly in terms of mastery versus relative performance. They state that when mastery is the goal (the criterion-referenced concept in which student performance is compared against a clear criterion or objective), learners are concerned with developing new skills, they value the learning process, and they believe that mastery depends on effort. When mastery is the goal, students like the class more and believe that effort and success go together. This constellation of attitudes is highly motivating.

On the other hand, when relative performance is the goal (the norm-referenced concept or comparing one student's performance against that of other students), learners are concerned with being judged able, they value normatively high outcomes, and they believe that ability is shown by success, outperforming others, and achieving success with little effort. When relative performance is the primary goal, students judge their ability lower and implicate their low ability as a cause of failure; such a perspective reflects a maladaptive motivational pattern. Ames and Archer concluded that a mastery structure, not a performance framework, is likely to develop long-term use of learning strategies. A mastery structure also helps students form realistic but challenging goals and encourages them to hold the helpful belief that success is related to one's own efforts.

Implications of the mastery model

The L2 classroom must focus on clear criteria (goals, standards) for students to master rather than on comparing one student's performance against the performance of others. This mastery approach supports the importance of goal-setting as a motivational factor. The mastery approach is much more positive than the relative performance approach in terms of students' beliefs in their own abilities and in their use of L2 learning strategies. The mastery model encourages risk-taking, participation, and involvement, all of which lead to greater proficiency in the target language. Serious competition (fostered by repeated comparisons of student performance) is not a particularly useful vehicle for L2 learning, although entertaining games and other forms of light competition can be good. The key lies in the classroom climate, which should be nonthreatening and positive at all times.

Non developmental motivation theories have been the focus of our discussion to this point. Now let us move to cognitive developmental and sociocultural theories, where Piaget and Vygotsky enlighten our understanding of motivation.

COGNITIVE DEVELOPMENTAL AND SOCIOCULTURAL THEORIES

Two theorists, Piaget and Vygotsky, offer ideas that broaden the theory of motivation. Theirs are very different contributions, one focusing on cognitive developmental aspects and the other on sociocultural elements.

Piaget's contributions

Piaget, born in Switzerland, wrote a book entitled *The Construction of Reality in the Child* (1954), which set the pace for generations of researchers. In his own mind, Piaget considered himself a philosopher rather than a psychologist, and he studied stages of child development to establish a theory of knowledge. He envisaged his contribution as mainly in logic and "genetic epistemology" (origins of knowledge), not in child development or education. Piaget's investigatory technique was mainly the intensive case study. He put his child subjects through many creative tasks that indicated their individual stages of cognitive development, according to his own highly detailed developmental system (Piaget, 1979). However, Piaget did not do research in classrooms full of children, nor did he expect his ideas to be applied to such classrooms. He actually took pains to avoid discussing educational applications of his research.

According to Piaget, children are motivated to develop their cognitive or mental abilities in a predictable set of stages: sensorimotor, preoperational, concrete operational, and formal operational. In these stages children move to accommodate their cognitive structures (*schemata*) to new stimuli or assimilate the new stimuli into their existing schemata. Motivation, then, is a built-in striving toward more complex and differentiated development of the individual's mental structures. A rich, stimulating environment enables the learner to develop cognitively, and a deprived environment stunts this development. Piaget underscored the importance of the earliest stages of cognitive development; if these were not achieved successfully, the person could not move ahead intellectually. Fulfillment of the previous stage, according to this model, is necessary for advancement to the next stage. Children's biological development occurs through organization and adaptation to the environment, and the same occurs for cognitive development, according to Piaget.

In Piaget's theory, an event does not become "internalized" by individuals. Instead, people construct knowledge according to the organization of the cognitive system. Kamii, Lewis, and Jones (1991) state that Piaget's theory and research demonstrate "that children acquire concepts by *constructing them from the inside*, in interaction with the environment, rather than by *internalizing* them from the environment" (p. 19). The term "acquisition" so often used in educational writings (as in skill acquisition, second language acquisition, or concept acquisition) has a flavor of "internalization" of something from the outside and thus contradicts Piagetian norms. Acquisition suggests an acquiring, an adding to, rather than the Piagetian idea of construction from within. "Discovery," another common educational term (as in discovery learning, the discovery stage in a lesson, or the discovery method of teaching), also does not seem to fit well with Piagetian theory, because it usually implies finding something that exists outside of oneself rather than constructing something from within.

Piaget's theory assumes that learners are creative, active, and participating. According to Kamii et al. (1991), learners do not simply observe objects in external reality (physical knowledge) or employ conventions worked out by people (social knowledge). Instead, learners also create or construct logico-mathematical knowledge, which is the knowledge of relationships among ideas, objects, people, and so on.

Some well-meaning followers of Piaget have bastardized his findings and his philosophy. Brown (1994) criticizes the warped oversimplification of Piagetian constructivism in curriculum design, a slant that encourages "sensitivity to what children of a certain age *cannot* do because they have not yet reached a certain stage of cognitive operations" (Brown, 1994, p. 10). No doubt Piaget would cringe if he could see his work iconified and applied in such a restrictive manner.

However, Yager (1991) provides a very helpful set of constructivist teaching techniques based on Piagetian ideas. Among these techniques are: (1) seeking out and using student questions to guide lessons, (2) accepting and encouraging student initiation of ideas, (3) promoting student self-regulation and action, (4) using students' experiences and interests to drive lessons (and thus offering multiple branches for learning), (5) encouraging uses of alternative sources of information, (6) using open-ended questions and encouraging student elaboration when possible, (7) encouraging students to suggest causes for events and situations and to predict consequences, (8) seeking out student ideas before presenting ideas from the text, (9) allowing adequate time for reflection and analysis, (10) facilitating reformulation of ideas in light of new experiences and evidence, and (11) encouraging social interaction. Brown (1992) contrasts the traditional classroom to what she calls an "intentional learning environment," which reflects Piagetian ideas and includes students as active researchers, teachers, and self-monitors; teachers as guiders of discovery and as models of inquiry; thinking as basic literacy; depth, themes, coherence, and understanding of content; use of technology for reflection and collaboration; and authentic assessment through performance, projects, and portfolios.

Implications of Piaget's work

Piaget's work suggests that learning a new language, like learning one's native language, is part of the individual's progress toward cognitive development. Language development (in the native language or a second or a foreign language) deserves and requires a stimulating environment; without this kind of environment, the individual's inborn, motivated quest for cognitive growth will be hindered. The nature of L2 learning motivation might change over time in a developmental way.

The typical foreign language classroom in which communication is teacher-to-student is not usually the kind of stimulating place that Piaget had in mind; on the other hand, innovative, communicative foreign language classrooms offer a quantum leap in terms of richness and variety of language stimulation. By their very nature second language environments are much better at providing exceptionally rich input for learners, and foreign language teachers should, whenever possible, draw ideas, materials, and inspiration from second language settings.

Another hint arises from considering Piaget's research: the importance of early development in infancy and childhood. Learners of a new language — if expected to attain fluency and natural pronunciation — would be far better off to start the language in their early years, rather than waiting until adolescence or adulthood (Scarcella and Oxford, 1992). Young students are often highly motivated, especially because they can see clear progress in development of fluency and pronunciation.

Vygotsky's contributions

Vygotsky, a Russian psychologist, offers contributions in the realm of sociocultural cognition. According to his theory, an individual's cognitive system is a direct result of interaction in social groups and cannot be separated from social life (Vygotsky, 1987; Chaika, 1982). Group learning, where pairs and small groups of students learn together through social interaction, is one of Vygotsky's recommendations, although there is also much interaction between the individual learner and the teacher. The teacher acts as a facilitator or guide. When the learner needs the greatest assistance, the teacher provides "scaffolding" to ensure that the learner's constructs will continue to grow stronger and more complex. As the learner requires less help, the teacher slowly removes the no longer needed scaffolding that props up the learner, and the learner becomes increasingly self-directed and self-empowered.

The concept of scaffolding is directly linked to the idea of the zone of proximal development, defined as the distance between the learner's actual developmental level and the level of potential development (Vygotsky, 1978). The learner progresses through three stages: (1) assistance is provided by the teacher or more capable peers, (2) assistance is provided by oneself (self-correction, self-direction), and (3) no need of assistance at all because the knowledge is automatic. The scaffolding is gradually removed in Stages Two and Three. Brown (1994) emphasizes that the classroom should contain multiple zones of proximal development, since learners have different rates of development and are not cut from a single "cookie-cutter." Brown also highlights the need for a community of learners, which was developed by Rogoff (1994).

Tharp and Gallimore (1988) state that clear, valued goals are essential in moving students through the zone of proximal development toward their best proficiency. "It is only the goal-driven activity that makes the maximum contribution of each individual desirable to the entire group, thus motivating assistance..." (Tharp and Gallimore, 1988, p. 73). Students' goals and interests must be the starting point if motivation is to be high and developmental progress is to occur. Moreover, for motivation and progress to exist, instructional input to students must be challenging and relevant.

Vygotsky also provides another important concept: private speech, which mediates mental processes such as voluntary attention, logical problem-solving, planning, evaluation, voluntary memory, and intentional learning (Lantolf, 1994). "Symbolic mediation" is the term for this use of private speech. McCafferty (1994) explains that private speech has metacognitive, cognitive, social, and affective functions or purposes. Wertsch (1985) categorizes private speech into three divisions: object-regulation, self-regulation, and other-regulation.

Implications of Vygotsky's work

Vygotsky's work implies that L2 learning goals must be clearly based on learners' needs and interests for motivation to occur, and the input from the teacher must be both relevant and demanding. If these stipulations are not met, progress through the zone of proximal development will be stunted. The great significance of the teacher as the provider of assistance to language learners is emphasized in the first stage of L2 learning.

Private speech is potentially important in the L2 field, so much so that an entire special issue of the 1994 *Modern Language Journal* is devoted to Vygotsky's private speech concepts. In that issue, Donato and McCormick argue that L2 learning strategies cannot be taught but are instead a by-product of mediational private speech, which they contend is closely linked to the formation of clear, specific L2 learning goals that spark motivation. This assertion of the nonteachability of L2 learning strategies is contradicted by years of strategy instruction research (Oxford, 1990b). Nevertheless, Donato and McCormick are on the right track in underscoring the importance of private speech in goal-setting, which, incidentally, is a teachable learning strategy and a strong motivational tool. Appel and Lantolf (1994) show that private speech can be used to aid both native language (L1) and L2 memory in text recall tasks.

SUMMARY OF IMPLICATIONS FOR TEACHERS OF A BROADER FRAMEWORK FOR L2 LEARNING MOTIVATION

We are offering here the important start of an expanded model of L2 learning motivation that enhances and enlarges the prevalent social psychological theory in useful ways. The basis for an expanded theory comes from the principles discussed throughout this article, drawn not just from social psychology but also from general, industrial, educational, cognitive developmental, and sociocultural psychology. The broader framework toward which we are working does not obviate Gardner's theory of L2 learning motivation. Instead, the broader framework includes other possible motivations and additional mechanisms by which these motivations become reflected in students' behaviors.

The following is a summary of practical implications for L2 teachers based on a synthesis of all the relevant theories of motivation mentioned here. Some implications might seem like common sense, and others might appear quite new to many teachers. All of these recommendations would benefit from L2 research.

First, teachers can identify why students are studying the new language. Integrative and instrumental reasons are likely to be among the frequently mentioned motivators, but the language requirement is a definite motivator also. Other possible reasons are many and varied: cultural curiosity, travel interests (which might not always involve integrative motives), altruism, and intellectual challenge. Teachers can recognize that foreign and second language learners probably have different clusters of motivations, although they share the same basic emotional needs for comfort, acceptance, and esteem. Teachers can find out what students' actual motivations are by giving a motivation survey or discussing students' motivations at the beginning of each term (or at other times as needed). Teachers can be aware that over time, students' motivations might change developmentally in kind and degree, so asking students periodically is a good idea. Information on motivation (as well as language performance) can be passed along in an individual portfolio to the next language teacher for planning purposes. To encourage the highest possible motivation, each teacher can determine which parts of L2 learning (e.g., speaking conversationally, listening to lectures in the L2, reading L2 newspapers) are especially valuable to the students and can plan activities that include those aspects.

Second, teachers can help shape their students' beliefs about success or failure in L2 learning. Teachers can inculcate the belief that success is not only possible but probable, as long as there is a high level of effort. This positive set of attitudes is related to the setting of reasonable but challenging goals and subgoals. Students can learn to have realistic but challenging goals regarding their eventual proficiency and can develop immediate, achievable subgoals that give them a sense of progress. Teachers can help students meet these aims through private speech and through learner training in goal-setting and self-assessment. Teachers can also learn to accept varied goals and provide appropriate feedback on those goals. Some students have more ambitious goals than others. Some students want and expect to develop high levels of proficiency in speaking, others simply want to develop passable reading skills, and still others just want to meet the language requirement and turn to other subjects. Teachers can also accept diversity in the way students establish and meet their goals based on differences in learning styles: visual, auditory, hands-on; reflective, impulsive; extroverted, introverted; closure-oriented, open. Because students' aims and means of achieving those aims are variable, variety in instructional content, pacing, grouping, and materials is to be encouraged.

Third, teachers can help students heighten their motivation by demonstrating that L2 learning can be an exciting mental challenge, a career enhancer, a vehicle to cultural awareness and friendship, and a key to world peace. Teachers can provide evidence that the benefits of L2 learning are truly worth the costs. Teachers can invite former students to the class to show the rewards of L2 learning. Teachers can also invite visitors who are native speakers of the L2 to share cultural information and to confirm that the students can really use the language communicatively.

Fourth, teachers can make the L2 classroom a welcoming, positive place where psychological needs are met and where language anxiety is kept to a minimum. Teachers can provide appropriate instructional features. Some characteristics of optimal L2 instruction, according to our expanded theory, include variety, clear and important activities, appropriate feedback, L2 assistance tailored to learners' specific needs, and (especially for internally directed learners) the chance for self-direction. L2 tasks can lead to success and must be perceived as valuable and relevant. They can offer richness of stimulation by recreating realistic situations where use of the language is essential (e.g., traveling, ordering meals, finding a doctor, going shopping, solving a problem). Teachers can go beyond survival communication through ingenious language tasks (e.g., surveying native speakers in the community for an opinion poll, inviting native speakers to participate in class discussions and debates, taking field trips involving use of the language, using increasingly challenging information-gap activities and simulations).

Fifth, extrinsic rewards provided by the teacher are part of the L2 instructional design, but teachers can also urge students to develop their own intrinsic rewards through positive self-talk (a form of private speech) and through guided self-evaluation. Teachers can help students build their own intrinsic reward system by emphasizing mastery of specific goals, not comparison with other students. Teachers can thus enable students to have an increased sense of self-efficacy, whereby they attribute the outcome to their own efforts rather than to the behaviors of teachers or other students. Greater self-efficacy increases motivation to continue learning the L2.

RESEARCH RECOMMENDATIONS

Research is essential on all the key instructional recommendations given above. Some of these suggestions have been studied in the L2 field, but not adequately. Others have not been examined at all within the L2 arena. Surely a careful look at each of the main instructional recommendations would be valuable.

Research on L2 learning motivation should be conducted longitudinally, not just cross-sectionally. Longitudinal investigations allow the tracking of motivation over time for the same individuals, and the results of such research give us developmental data on changes in motivation (intensity and type). At this stage, all we have are anecdotes regarding alterations in motivation. These stories, while interesting, do not provide adequate data on which to make general statements about how learners' motivations wax and wane — and sometimes wax again. The anecdotes also fail to provide wide-scale data on how learners change their specific motivational orientations (goals or reasons for learning the L2) over time.

Another research recommendation concerns the overall design of any investigation involving motivation. Such an investigation must involve a multifactorial view of motivation. That is, the construct of motivation cannot revolve around one simple idea, such as expectancy; the construct must be broad and have many component parts (as discussed in Chapter 2, this volume). Below are some of the variables that the design must include. Note that sometimes a variable is repeated, because it issues from several sources.

General variables:

- L2 aptitude
- Gender
- Age
- Cultural and family background
- Language spoken at home
- Previous L2 learning experience (where, when, what, and attitudes toward)

Variables from Crookes and Schmidt:

- Interest in the L2
- Relevance of learning the L2 (perceptions of needs such as achievement, affiliation, and power)
- Expectancy of success or failure
- Outcomes (rewards)
- Decision to participate in L2 learning
- Perseverance or persistence
- Maintenance of a high activity level

Variables from Dörnyei:

- Intrinsic and extrinsic rewards
- Goal-setting
- Attribution theory
- Learned helplessness
- Self-efficacy
- Self-confidence
- Need for achievement

- Anxiety
- Course-, teacher-, and group-specific aspects

Variables from Gardner's social psychological theory:

- Nature of the motivational orientation (goal)
- Attitude toward the L2 community (integrativeness)
- Degree of general interest in languages and cultures (integrativeness)
- Attitudes toward the current L2 learning experience (toward teacher, course, setting, materials, methods, etc.)
- Effort (motivational intensity)
- Desire to learn the language (valence)
- Attitude toward learning the L2

Variables from need theories:

- Degree of need for achievement (and possibly fear of failure)
- Degree of success-avoidance
- Presence of learner satisfaction elements, such as variety, clarity and importance of tasks, autonomy, and feedback

Variables from instrumentality (expectancy-value) theories:

- Degree of expectancy of success in L2 learning
- Amount of value offered by success in L2 learning
- Clarity of L2 learning goals
- Difficulty of L2 learning goals
- Degree of personal responsibility in setting L2 learning goals
- Effort to achieve L2 learning goals

Variables from equity theories:

- Perceived inputs (effort, experience, skills, ability, seniority, etc.)
- Perceived L2 outcomes
- Ratio of perceived inputs to perceived L2 outcomes (equitable or inequitable ratio)

Variables from reinforcement theories:

- L2 motivated behaviors (effort and success)
- Rewards contingent on the occurrence of specific behaviors
- Rewards not contingent on behaviors

Variables from industrial psychology and social cognition:

- Commitment to L2 goals
- Feedback on goal-related performance
- Ability or aptitude in relation to L2 goals
- Amount and kind of role-modeling in or outside of the L2 classroom

- Rewards (intrinsic and extrinsic)
- Self-efficacy
- Attribution
- Persistence, effort, and strategy use

Variables from the mastery model:

- Classroom orientation: norm-referenced (relative performance) versus criterion-referenced (mastery)
- Risk-taking
- Participation and involvement

Variables from cognitive developmental theory:

- Stages of L2 learning (including changes in L2 motivation)
- Ability of the L2 learner to construct concepts creatively instead of internalizing them
- Degree and kind of cognitive and social stimulation in the learning environment
- Participation and involvement

Variables from sociocultural theory:

- Clarity of the learner's L2 goals
- Perceived value of the learner's L2 goals
- Use of private speech as a goal-setting tool
- Degree to which learner's interests and goals are taken into account
- Degree of assistance from the teacher or others to help learners move along the zone of proximal development

Quite clearly, L2 learning motivation is a complex, multifaceted phenomenon. It does not defy researchers, but it challenges them mightily to look beyond simple explanations. Of greatest note to L2 learning motivation investigators are the following crucial variables culled from the lists above. These variables must be part of any model of language learning motivation.

1. *Attitudes.* Attitudes toward the L2 community, the language, the teacher, the course, and the L2 learning environment;

2. *Beliefs about self.* Beliefs or expectancies about one's own ability to succeed in learning the L2, based on previous experiences and on attitudes about oneself as a learner (including self-confidence, attributions, self-efficacy, and anxiety);

3. *Goals.* Content, clarity, and perceived value of goals held by the L2 learner and how those goals were established (by learner, teacher, institution, or other), where goals are defined as motivational orientation/reason;

4. *Involvement.* Creative, active, persevering participation of the learner in the L2 learning process;

5. *Assistance/Environment.* Degree of teacher- or peer-provided assistance in a community of L2 learners, and the nature of the learning environment and the institutional and cultural environment;

6. *Performance links.* The relationship between varieties of L2 motivation and L2 performance; and

7. *Demographics/personal.* Aptitude, age, sex, previous languages learned, language spoken at home, travel experiences, family characteristics.

CONCLUSION

L2 learning is a complex process is which motivation plays a major role. The prevalent concept of L2 learning motivation, while important and extremely useful, can be expanded to include a greater range of motivations present in learners. Contributions from many aspects of psychology — general, industrial, educational, cognitive developmental, and sociocultural — are helpful for an expanded vision of L2 learning motivation. Here we offer the beginnings of an expanded model. L2 learners and teachers alike will benefit from the development of these beginnings into a complete model through wide-ranging discussion, debate, and empirical research.

NOTE

Portions of this paper were published in an article in *Modern Language Journal* (1994, 78, 12–28) entitled "Language Learning Motivation: Expanding the Theoretical Framework," by Rebecca Oxford and Jill Shearin. Other sections contain new, unpublished material.

REFERENCES

Adams, J. S. (1965). Inequity in social exchange. In L. Berkowitz (Ed.), *Advances in experimental social psychology* (Vol. 2). New York: Academic Press.

Adams, J. S. (1975). Inequity in social exchange. In R. M. Steers & L. W. Porter (Eds.), *Motivation and work behavior*. New York: McGraw-Hill.

Alderfer, C. P. (1969). An empirical test of a new theory of human needs. *Organizational Behavior and Human Performance, 4,* 142–175.

Alderfer, C. P. (1972). *Existence, relatedness, and growth: Human needs in organizational settings.* New York: Free Press.

Ames, C. (1984). Competitive, cooperative, and individual goal structures: A cognitive-motivational analysis. In R. E. Ames & C. E. Ames (Eds.), *Research on motivation: Student motivation* (Vol. 1, pp. 177–207). San Diego: Academic Press.

Ames, C. (1992). Classrooms: Goals, structures, and student motivation. *Journal of Educational Psychology, 84,* 261–271. .

Ames, C., & Archer, J. (1988). Achievement goals in the classroom: Students' learning strategies and motivation process. *Journal of Educational Psychology, 80,* 260–267.

Appel, G., & Lantolf, J. P. (1994). Speaking as mediation: A study of L1 and L2 text recall tasks. *Modern Language Journal, 78,* 437–452.

Arnold, H. J. (1976). Effects of performance feedback and extrinsic reward upon high intrinsic motivation. *Organizational Behavior and Human Performance, 17,* 275–288.

Atkinson, J. W. (1964). *An introduction to motivation.* Princeton, NJ: Van Nostrand.

Atkinson, J. W. (1974). Strength of motivation and efficiency of performance. In J. W. Atkinson & J. O. Raynor (Eds.), *Motivation and achievement* (pp. 117–142). New York: V. W. Winston.

Au, S. Y. (1988). A critical appraisal of Gardner's socio-psychological theory of second-language (L2) learning. *Language Learning, 38,* 75–100.

Bagnole, J. W. (1993). The magic and mystery of motivation in TEFL and language learning. *TESOL Matters, February/March,* 10.

Bandura, A. (1978). The self system in reciprocal determinism. *American Psychologist, 33,* 344–358.

Bandura, A. (1982). Self-efficacy mechanism in human agency. *American Psychologist, 37,* 122–147.

Bandura, A., & Cervone, D. (1986). Differential engagement of self-reactive influences in cognitive motivation. *Organizational Behavior and Human Decision Processes, 38*, 92–113.

Bandura, A., & Shunk, D. H. (1981). Cultivating competence, self-efficacy, and intrinsic interest through proximal self-motivation. *Journal of Personality and Social Psychology, 41*, 586–598.

Bardwell, R., & Braaksma, E. F. (1983). Motivation as a multifactor trait. *Journal of Psychology, 119*, 5–14.

Boekaerts, M. (1987). Individual differences in the appraisal of learning tasks: An integrative view on emotion and cognition. *Communication and Cognition, 20*, 207–224.

Boekaerts, M. (1989). Motivated learning: Bias in appraisals. *International Journal of Educational Research, 12*, 267–280.

Bretz, M. L., Dvorak, T., & Kirschner, C. (1992). *Pasajes.* New York: McGraw-Hill.

Brindley, G. (1989). The role of needs analysis in adult ESL programme design. In R. K. Johnson (Ed.), *The second language curriculum* (pp. 63–78). Cambridge: Cambridge University Press.

Brown, A. L. (1992). Design experiments: Theoretical and methodological challenges in creating complex interventions in classroom settings. *Journal of the Learning Sciences, 2*, 141–178.

Brown, A. L. (1994). The advancement of learning. *Educational Researcher, 23*, 4–12.

Brown, H. D. (1987). *Principles of language learning and teaching* (2nd edition). Englewood Cliffs, NJ: Prentice Hall.

Brown, H. D. (1990). M&Ms for language classrooms? Another look at motivation. In J. E. Alatis (Ed.), *Georgetown University Round Table on Language and Linguistics* (pp. 383–393). Washington, DC: Georgetown University Press.

Brown, H. D. (1994). *Teaching by principles.* Englewood Cliffs, NJ: Prentice Hall.

Burnaby, B., and Sun, Y. (1989). Chinese teachers' view of Western language teaching: Context informs paradigms. *TESOL Quarterly, 23*, 219–238.

Campbell, C. (1987). *Survey of attitudes specific to the foreign language classroom.* Unpublished manuscript.

Carr, T. H., & Curran, T. (1994). Cognitive factors in learning about structured sequences: Applications to syntax. *Studies in Second Language Acquisition, 16*, 205–230.

Carroll, J. B. (1963). A model of school learning. *Teacher's College Record, 64*, 723–733.

Carroll, J. B., & Sapon, S. M. (1959). *Modern Language Aptitude Test*. New York: Psychological Corporation.

Castanell, L. (1984). A cross-cultural look at achievement motivation research. *Journal of Negro Education, 53*, 435–443.

Celce-Murcia, M., & Hilles, S. (1988). *Techniques and resources in teaching grammar*. Oxford: Oxford University Press.

Chaika, E. (1982). *Language: The social mirror*. Cambridge, MA: Newbury House.

Christensen, L., & Ehrman, M. (1993). *Language learning motivation and strategies questionnaire*. Unpublished manuscript.

Clark, J. (1986). *A study of the comparability of speaking proficiency across three government language training agencies*. Washington, DC: Center for Applied Linguistics.

Clément, R. (1980). Ethnicity, contact and communicative competence in a second language. In H. Giles, W. P. Robinson & P. M. Smith (Eds.), *Language: Social psychological perspectives* (pp. 147–154). Oxford: Pergamon.

Clément, R., Dörnyei, Z., & Noels, K. A. (1994). Motivation, self-confidence, and group cohesion in the foreign language classroom. *Language Learning, 44*, 417–448.

Clément, R., & Kruidenier, B. G. (1985). Aptitude, attitude and motivation in second language proficiency: A test of Clément's model. *Journal of Language and Social Psychology, 4*, 21–37.

Clément, R., Major, L., Gardner, R. C., & Smythe, P. C. (1977). Attitudes and motivation in second language acquisition: An investigation of Ontario francophones. *Working Papers in Bilingualism, 12*, 1–10.

Cohen, A. D. (1990). *Language learning: Insights for learners, teachers, and researchers*. New York: Newbury House/Harper & Row.

Cooley, W. W., & Leinhardt, F. (1975). *The application of a model for investigating classroom processes*. Pittsburgh: Learning Research and Development Center.

Crandall, V. J. (1963). Achievement. In H. W. Stevenson (Ed.), *Child Psychology: Sixty-Second Yearbook of the National Society for the Study of Education*. Chicago: University of Chicago Press.

Crandall, V. C., & Battle, E. S. (1970). The antecedents and adult correlates of academic and intellectual effort. In J. P. Hill (Ed.), *Minnesota Symposia on Child Psychology* (Vol. 4). Minnesota: University of Minnesota Press.

Crandall, V. J., Katovsky, W., & Preston, A. (1960). Parents' attitudes and behaviors and grade-school children's academic achievements. *Journal of Genetic Psychology, 104*, 53–66.

Crookall, D., & Oxford, R. L. (1990). *Simulation, gaming, and language learning*. New York: Newbury House/Harper & Row.

Crookes, G, & Schmidt, R. (1991). Motivation: Reopening the research agenda. *Language Learning, 41*, 469–512.

Csikszentmihalyi, M., & Nakamura, J. (1989). The dynamics of intrinsic motivation: A study of adolescents. In C. Ames & R. Ames (Eds.), *Research on motivation in education, (Vol. 3, Goals and cognitions*, pp. 44–71). San Diego: Academic Press.

Curry, B. (1990). *Motivation for learning a second or foreign language*. Unpublished manuscript. University of Alabama.

deCharms, R. (1968). *Personal causation: The internal affective determinants of behavior*. New York: Academic Press.

Deci, E. L. (1972). The effects of contingent and noncontingent rewards and controls on intrinsic motivation. *Organizational Behavior and Human Performance, 8*, 217–229.

Deci, E. L., & Ryan, R. M. (1985). *Intrinsic motivation and self-determination in human behavior*. New York: Plenum.

Deci, E. L., Vallerand, R. J., Pelletier, L. G., & Ryan, R. M. (1991). Motivation and education: The self-determination perspective. *Educational Psychologist, 26*, 325–346.

Donato, R., & McCormick, D. (1994). A sociocultural perspective on language learning strategies: The role of mediation. *Modern Language Journal, 78*, 453–464.

Dörnyei, Z. (1990a). Conceptualizing motivation in foreign-language learning. *Language Learning, 40*, 45–78.

Dörnyei, Z. (1990b, April). *Analysis of motivation components in foreign language learning*. Paper presented at the 9th World Congress of Applied Linguistics, Thessaloniki-Halkidiki, Greece. (ERIC Document Reproduction Service No. ED 323 810).

Dörnyei, Z. (1994a). Motivation and motivating in the foreign language classroom. *Modern Language Journal, 78*, 273–284.

Dörnyei, Z. (1994b). Understanding L2 motivation: On with the challenge! *Modern Language Journal, 78*, 515–523.

Duda, J. L., & Allison, M. T. (1989). The attributional theory of achievement motivation: Cross-cultural considerations. *International Journal of Intercultural Relations, 13*, 37–55.

Dweck, C. S., & Leggett, E. L. (1988). A social-cognitive approach to motivation and personality. *Psychological Review, 95*, 256–273.

Dyer, L., & Parker, D. F. (1975). Classifying outcomes in work motivation research: An examination of the intrinsic-extrinsic dichotomy. *Journal of Applied Psychology, 60,* 455–458.

Ehrman, M. E. (1993). Ego boundaries revisited: Toward a model of personality and learning. In J. E. Alatis (Ed.), *Strategic interaction and language acquisition: Theory, practice, and research* (pp. 331–362). Washington, DC: Georgetown University Press.

Ehrman, M. E. (1994a). The Type Differentiation Indicator and adult language learning success. *Journal of Psychological Type, 30,* 10–29.

Ehrman, M. E. (1994b). Weakest and strongest learners in intensive language training: A study of extremes. In C. Klee (Ed.), *Faces in a crowd: Individual learners in multisection programs* (pp. 81–118). Boston: Heinle & Heinle.

Ehrman, M. E. (in press). Personality, language learning aptitude, and program structure. In J. Alatis (Ed.), *Linguistics and the education of second language teachers: Ethnolinguistic, psycholinguistic, and sociolinguistic aspects.* Washington DC: Georgetown University Press.

Ehrman, M. E., & Jackson, F. H. (1992). *Classroom activities survey.* Unpublished manuscript.

Ehrman, M. E., & Oxford, R. L. (1989). Effects of sex differences, career choice, and psychological type on adults' language learning strategies. *Modern Language Journal, 73,* 1–13.

Ehrman, M. E., & Oxford, R. L. (1990). Adult language learning styles and strategies in an intensive training setting. *Modern Language Journal, 74,* 311–327.

Ehrman, M. E., & Oxford, R. L. (1991). *Affective survey.* Unpublished manuscript. Arlington, VA: Foreign Service Institute.

Ehrman, M. E., & Oxford, R. L. (1995). Cognition plus: Correlates of language learning success. *Modern Language Journal, 79,* 67–89.

Ely, C. (1986a). An analysis of discomfort, risktaking, sociability, and motivation in the L2 classroom. *Language Learning, 36,* 1–25.

Ely, C. (1986b). Language learning motivation: A descriptive and causal analysis. *Modern Language Journal, 70,* 28–35.

Fotos, S. (1994). Motivation in second language learning pedagogy: A critical review. *Senshu University Bulletin of the Humanities, 24,* 29–54.

Frank, C., & Rinvolucri, M. (1983). *Grammar in action: Awareness activities for language learning.* Oxford: Pergamon.

Gallagher, J. J. (1994). Teaching and learning: New models. In L. W. Porter, & M. W. Rosenzweig (Eds.), *Annual Review of Psychology, 45,* 171–195.

Gardner, R. C. (1985a). *Motivation questionnaire*. Unpublished manuscript.

Gardner, R. C. (1985b). *Social psychology and language learning: The role of attitudes and motivation*. London, Ontario: Edward Arnold.

Gardner, R. C. (1988). The socio-educational model of second-language learning: assumptions, findings, and issues. *Language Learning, 38*, 101–126.

Gardner, R. C., & Clément, R. (1990). Social psychological perspectives on second language acquisition. In H. Giles & W. P. Robinson (Eds.), *Handbook of language and social psychology* (pp. 495–517). London: John Wiley.

Gardner, R. C., Lalonde, R. N., Moorcroft, R., & Evers, F. T. (1985). *Second language attrition: The role of motivation and use* (Research Bulletin 638). London, Ontario: University of Western Ontario, Department of Psychology.

Gardner, R. C., & Lambert, W. E. (1959). Motivational variables in second language acquisition. *Canadian Journal of Psychology, 13*, 266–272.

Gardner, R. C., & Lambert, W. E. (1972). *Attitudes and motivation in second language learning*. Rowley, MA: Newbury House.

Gardner, R. C., & Lambert, W. E. (1975). *Second language acquisition: A social-psychological approach* (Research Bulletin No. 332). London, Ontario: University of Western Ontario, Department of Psychology.

Gardner, R. C., & MacIntyre, P. D. (1991). An instrumental motivation in language study: Who says it isn't effective? *Studies in Second Language Acquisition, 13*, 57–72.

Gardner, R. C., & MacIntyre, P. D. (1993). A student's contributions to second-language learning. Part II: Affective variables. *Language Teaching, 26*, 1–11.

Gardner, R. C., & Smythe, P. C. (1975). Motivation and second-language acquisition. *Canadian Modern Language Review, 3*, 218–233.

Gardner, R. C., & Tremblay, P. F. (1994a). On motivation, research agendas, and theoretical frameworks. *Modern Language Journal, 78*, 359–368.

Gardner, R. C., & Tremblay, P. F. (1994b). On motivation: Measurement and conceptual considerations. *Modern Language Journal, 78*, 524–527.

Genesee, F. (1978). *Is there an optimal age for starting second language instruction?* Unpublished manuscript, McGill University, Montréal, Québec, Canada.

Genesee, F., & Hamayan, E. (1980). Individual differences in second language learning. *Applied Psycholinguistics 1*, 95–110.

Georgopolis, B. S., Mahoney, G. M., & Jones, N. W. (1951). A path-goal approach to productivity. *Journal of Applied Psychology, 41*, 345–353.

Giles, H., & Byrne, J. L. (1982). An intergroup approach to second language acquisition. *Journal of Multicultural and Multilingual Development, 3,* 7–40.

Gliksman, L., Gardner, R. C., & Smythe, P. C. (1982). The role of the integrative motive on students' participation in the French classroom. *Canadian Modern Language Review, 38,* 625–647.

Gist, M. E., Schwoerer, C., & Rosen, B. (1989). Effectiveness of alternative training methods on self-efficacy and performance in computer software training. *Journal of Applied Psychology, 74,* 884–891.

Gottfried, A. E. (1985). Academic intrinsic motivation in elementary and junior high school students. *Journal of Educational Psychology, 77,* 631–645.

Guiora, A. Z. (1984). The dialect of language acquisition. *Language Learning, 34,* 3–12.

Hackman, J. R., & Oldham, G. R. (1975). Development of the job diagnostic survey. *Journal of Applied Psychology, 60,* 159–170.

Hackman, J. R., & Oldham, G. R. (1976). Motivation through the design of work: Test of a theory. *Organizational Behavior and Human Performance, 16,* 250–279.

Hall, D. T., & Nougain, K. E. (1968). An examination of Maslow's need hierarchy in an organizational setting. *Organizational Behavior and Human Performance, 3,* 12–35.

Hart-Gonzalez, L. H., & Ehrman, M. E. (1992). *Study activities questionnaire.* Unpublished manuscript.

Hartmann, E. (1991). *Boundaries in the mind: A new psychology of personality.* New York: Basic Books.

Hatch, E., & Lazaraton, A. (1991). *The research manual: Design and statistics for applied linguistics.* New York: Newbury House.

Heider, F. (1958). *The psychology of interpersonal relationships.* New York: Wiley.

Herzberg, F. (1966). *Work and the nature of man.* Cleveland: World Publishing.

Horner, M. S. (1968). *Sex differences in achievement motivation and performance in competitive and noncompetitive situations.* Unpublished doctoral dissertation, University of Michigan, Ann Arbor.

Horner, M. S. (1970). The motive to avoid success and changing aspirations of college women. In J. M. Bardwick (Ed.), *Readings on the Psychology of Women* (pp. 62–67). New York: Harper & Row.

Horwitz, E. K. (1985). Using student beliefs about language learning and teaching in the foreign language methods course. *Foreign Language Annals, 18,* 333–340.

Horwitz, E. K. (1986). Preliminary evidence for the reliability and validity of a foreign language anxiety scale. *TESOL Quarterly, 20,* 559–562.

Horwitz, E. K. (1990). Attending to the affective domain in the foreign language classroom. In S. S. Magnan (Ed.), *Shifting the instructional focus to the learner* (pp. 15–33). Middlebury, VT: Northeast Conference on the Teaching of Foreign Languages.

Horwitz, E. K., Horwitz, M. B., & Cope, J. (1986). Foreign language classroom anxiety. *Modern Language Journal, 70,* 125–132.

Horwitz, E. K., & Young, D. J. (1991). *Language anxiety: From theory and research to classroom implications.* Englewood Cliffs, NJ: Prentice Hall.

Johnson, D. W. (1979). *Educational psychology.* Englewood Cliffs, NJ: Prentice Hall.

Jorden, E., & Noda, M. (1987). *Japanese: The spoken language.* New Haven: Yale University Press.

Julkunen, K. (1989). *Situation- and task-specific motivation in foreign-language learning and teaching* (Publications in Education No. 6). Joensuu, Finland: University of Joensuu.

Julkunen, K. (1991). Situation- and task-specific motivation in foreign-language learning and teaching. *Dissertation Abstracts International, 52,* 716C.

Kamii, C., Lewis, B. A., & Jones, S. (1991). Reform in primary mathematics education: A constructivist view. *Educational Horizons, 70,* 19–26.

Kanfer, R. (1990). Motivation and individual differences in learning: An integration of developmental, differential, and cognitive perspectives. *Learning and Individual Differences, 2,* 221–239.

Kanfer, R., & Ackerman, P. L. (1989). Motivation and cognition abilities: An integrative/aptitude-treatment interaction approach to skill acquisition [Monograph]. *Journal of Applied Psychology, 74,* 657–690.

Kashima, Y., & Triandis, H. C. (1986). The self-serving bias in attributions as a coping strategy: A cross-cultural study. *Journal of Cross-Cultural Psychology, 17,* 83–97.

Kassabgy, O. (1976). *Attitudes and motivation in foreign language learning: A study made on a sample of Egyptian adult learners.* Unpublished master's thesis, The American University in Cairo, Cairo, Egypt.

Keller, J. M. (1983). Motivational design of instruction. In C. M. Reigeluth (Ed.), *Instructional design theories and models* (pp. 386–433). Hillsdale, NJ: Erlbaum.

Kern, R. G. (1995). Students' and teachers' beliefs about language learning. *Foreign Language Annals, 28,* 71–92.

Komin, S. (1990). Culture and work-related values in Thai organizations. *International Journal of Psychology, 25,* 681–704.

Kraemer, R. (1993). Social psychological factors related to the study of Arabic among Israeli high school students: A test of Gardner's socioeducational model. *Studies in Second Language Acquisition, 15,* 83–104.

Krashen, S. D. (1981). *Second language acquisition and second language learning.* Oxford: Pergamon.

Krashen, S. D. (1982). *Principles and practice in second language acquisition.* Oxford: Pergamon.

Krashen, S. D. (1985). *The input hypothesis.* New York: Longman.

Kruskal, J. B., & Wish, M. (1978). *Multidimensional scaling.* Sage University Series on Quantitative Applications in the Social Sciences, no. 07–011. Beverly Hills, CA: Sage.

Labrie, N., & Clément, R. (1986). Ethnolinguistic vitality, self-confidence and second language proficiency: An investigation. *Journal of Multilingual and Multicultural Development, 7,* 269–282.

Lambert, W. E., Gardner, R. C., Barik, H. C., & Tunstall, K. (1963). Attitudinal and cognitive aspects of intensive study of a second language. *Journal of Abnormal and Social Psychology, 66,* 358–368.

Landy, F. (1985). *Psychology of work behavior.* Homewood, IL: Dorsey Press.

Lantolf, J. P. (1994). Sociocultural theory and second language learning. *Modern Language Journal, 78,* 418–420.

Lavine, R. Z., & Oxford, R. L. (1990). *Addressing affective factors in the second and foreign language classroom.* Paper presented at the annual meeting of the Modern Language Association, Chicago, IL.

Lawler, E. E., & Suttle, J. L. (1972). A causal-correlational test of the need hierarchy concept. *Organizational Behavior and Human Performance, 7,* 265–287.

Lens, W., & DeCruyenaere, M. (1991). Motivation and de-motivation in secondary education: Student characteristics. *Learning and Instruction, 1,* 145–159.

Lepper, M. R., Aspinwall, L., Mumme, D., Chabay, R. W. (1992). Self-perception and social perception processes in tutoring: Subtle social control strategies of expert tutors. In J. Olson & M. P. Zanna (Eds.), *Self-inference Processes: The Sixth Ontario Symposium in Social Psychology.* Hillsdale, NJ: Erlbaum.

Lepper, M. R., & Greene, D. (1975). Turning play into work: Effects of adult surveillance and extrinsic rewards on children's intrinsic motivation. *Journal of Personality and Social Psychology, 31,* 479–486.

Lepper, M. R., & Greene, D. (1978). *The hidden costs of reward: New perspectives on the psychology of human motivation.* Hillsdale, NJ: Erlbaum.

Locke, E. A. (1976). The nature and causes of job satisfaction. In M. D. Dunnette (Ed.), *Handbook of Industrial and Organizational Psychology*. Chicago: Rand McNally.

Locke, E. A. (1980). Latham versus Komaki: A tale of two paradigms. *Journal of Applied Psychology, 65*, 16–23.

Locke, E. A., & Latham, G. P. (1984). *Goal-setting*. Englewood Cliffs, NJ: Prentice Hall.

Locke, E. A., & Latham, G. P. (1990). Work motivation and satisfaction: Light at the end of the tunnel. *Psychological Science, 1*, 240–246.

Locke, E. A., Shaw, K. N., Saari, L. M., & Latham, G. P. (1981). Goal-setting and task performance: 1969–1980. *Psychological Bulletin, 90*, 125–152.

Logan, G. D. (1988). Toward an instance theory of automatization. *Psychological Review, 95*, 492–527.

MacIntyre, P. D., & Gardner, R. C. (1991a). Methods and results in the study of anxiety and language learning: a review of the literature. *Language Learning, 41*, 85–117.

MacIntyre, P. D., & Gardner, R. C. (1991b). Language anxiety: Its relationship to other anxieties and to processing in native and second languages. *Language Learning, 41*, 513–534.

Maehr, M. L., & Archer, J. (1987). Motivation and school achievement. In L. G. Katz (Ed.), *Current topics in early childhood education* (pp. 85–107). Norwood, NJ: Ablex.

Maehr, M. L., & Nicholls, J. G. (1980). Culture and achievement motivation: A second look. In N. Warren (Ed.), *Studies in cross-cultural psychology* (Vol. 2, pp. 221–267). New York: Academic Press.

Markus, H. R., & Kitayama, S. (1991). Culture and the self: Implications for cognition, emotion, and motivation. *Psychological Review, 98*, 224–253.

Maslow, A. H. (1970). *Motivation and personality*. New York: Harper & Row.

Matsui, T., Okada, A., & Mizuguchi, R. (1981). Expectancy theory prediction of the goal theory postulate, "The harder the goals, the higher the performance." *Journal of Applied Psychology, 66*, 54–58.

McCafferty, S. G. (1994). Adult second language learners' use of private speech: A review of studies. *Modern Language Journal, 78*, 421–436.

McClelland, D. C. (Ed.). (1955). *Studies in motivation*. New York: Appleton-Century-Crofts.

Mento, A. J., Cartledge, N. D., & Locke, E. A. (1980). Maryland vs. Michigan vs. Minnesota: Another look at the relationship of expectancy and goal difficulty to performance. *Organizational Behavior and Human Performance, 25*, 419–449.

Moskowitz, G. (1972). *Caring and sharing in the language classroom*. Rowley, MA: Newbury House.

Murphy-Berman, V., & Sharma, R. (1987). Testing the assumptions of attribution theory in India. *Journal of Social Psychology*, *126*, 607–616.

Murray, H. A. (1938). *Explorations in personality*. New York: Oxford University Press.

Myers, I. B., & McCaulley, M. H. (1985). *Manual: A guide to the development and use of the Myers-Briggs Type Indicator*. Palo Alto, CA: Consulting Psychologists Press.

Nicholls, J. G. (1984). Achievement motivation: Conceptions of ability, subjective experience, task choice, and performance. *Psychological Review*, *91*, 328–346.

Norusis, M. J. (1994). *SPSS for Windows 6.1*. Chicago, IL: SPSS Inc.

Nunan, D. (1989a). *Designing tasks for the communicative classroom*. Cambridge: Cambridge University Press.

Nunan, D. (1989b). Hidden agendas: The role of the learner in programme implementation. In R. K. Johnson (Ed.), *The second language curriculum* (pp. 176–186). Cambridge: Cambridge University Press.

Nyikos, M. (1987). *The effect of color and imagery as mnemonic strategies on learning and retention of lexical items in German*. Unpublished doctoral dissertation, Purdue University, West Lafayette, IN.

O'Bryen, P. (1995). *Methodological processes in motivation questionnaire development*. Unpublished manuscript, University of Hawai'i at Mānoa.

O'Malley, J. M., & Chamot, A. U. (1990). *Learning strategies in second language acquisition*. Cambridge: Cambridge University Press.

Oller, J. W. (1981). Research on affective variables: some remaining questions. In R. Andersen (Ed.), *New dimensions in second language acquisition research* (pp. 14–27). Rowley, MA: Newbury House.

Oller, J. W., & Perkins, K. (1980). Intelligence and language proficiency as sources of variance in self-reported affective variables. *Language Learning*, *28*, 85–97.

Omaggio Hadley, A. C. (1993). *Teaching language in context: Proficiency-oriented instruction*. Boston: Heinle & Heinle.

Oxford, R. L. (1989). Use of language learning strategies: A synthesis of studies with implications for strategy training. *System*, *17*, 235–247.

Oxford, R. L. (1990a). *Language learning strategies: What every teacher should know*. New York: Newbury House/Harper & Row.

Oxford, R. L. (1990b). Styles, strategies, and aptitude: Important connections for language learners. In T. S. Parry & C. W. Stansfield (Eds.), *Language aptitude reconsidered* (pp. 67–125). Englewood Cliffs, NJ: Prentice Hall.

Oxford, R. L. (1990c). Language learning strategies and beyond: A look at strategies in the context of styles. In S. S. Magnan (Ed.), *Shifting the instructional focus to the learner* (pp. 35–55). Middlebury, VT: Northeast Conference on the Teaching of Foreign Languages.

Oxford, R. L. (1992). *US and Japanese educational systems: Implications for global business — A view from this side of the ocean.* Presentation at the Annual Alabama Sakura Festival, Tuscaloosa, AL.

Oxford, R. L. (1993). Research on second language learning strategies. *Annual Review of Applied Linguistics, 13,* 175–187.

Oxford, R. L. (1994). Where are we with language learning motivation? *Modern Language Journal, 78,* 512–514.

Oxford, R. L. (1995). Gender differences in language learning styles: What do they mean? In J. Reid (Ed.), *Learning styles in the ESL/EFL classroom* (pp. 34–46). Boston: Heinle & Heinle.

Oxford, R. L., & Burry-Stock, J. (1995). Assessing the use of language learning strategies worldwide with the ESL/EFL version of the Strategy Inventory for Language Learning. *System, 23,* 1–23.

Oxford, R. L., & Ehrman, M. E. (1993). Second language research on individual differences. In W. Grabe (Ed.), *Issues in second language teaching and learning, Annual Review of Applied Linguistics XIII,* 188–205.

Oxford, R. L., & Ehrman, M. E. (1995). Adults' language learning strategies in an intensive foreign language program in the United States. *System, 23,* 359–386.

Oxford, R. L., Ehrman, M. E., & Lavine, R. Z. (1991). Style wars: Teacher-student style conflicts in the language classroom. In S. S. Magnan (Ed.), *Challenges in the 1990s for college foreign language programs* (pp. 1–25). Boston: Heinle & Heinle.

Oxford, R. L., Hollaway, M., & Murillo, D. (1992). Language learning styles: Research and practical considerations for teaching in the multicultural tertiary ESL/EFL classroom. *System, 20,* 439–456.

Oxford, R. L., & Nyikos, M. (1989). Variables affecting choice of language learning strategies: A pilot study. *Modern Language Journal, 73,* 291–300.

Oxford, R. L., & Shearin, J. (1994). Language learning motivation: Expanding the theoretical framework. *Modern Language Journal, 78,* 12–28.

Piaget, J. (1954). *The construction of reality in the child.* New York: Basic Books.

Piaget, J. (1955). *The language and thought of the child.* New York: Meridian.

Piaget, J. (1979). *The development of thought*. New York: Viking Press.

Pintrich, P. (1988). A process-oriented view of student motivation and cognition. In J. S. Stark & L. A. Mets (Eds.), *Improving teaching and learning through research* (pp. 65–77). San Francisco: Jossey-Bass.

Pintrich, P. (1989). The dynamic interplay of student motivation and cognition in the college classroom. In M. Maehr & C. Ames (Eds.), *Advances in motivation and achievement* (Vol. 6: *Motivation enhancing environments*, pp. 117–160). Hillsdale, NJ: Erlbaum.

Pritchard, R. D. (1969). Equity theory: A review and critique. *Organizational Behavior and Human Performance, 4*, 176–211.

Ramage, K. (1990). Motivational factors and persistence in foreign language study. *Language Learning, 30*, 189–219.

Rauschenberger, J., Schmitt, N., & Hunter, J. E. (1980). A test of the need hierarchy concept by a Markov model of change in need strength. *Administrative Science Quarterly, 25*, 654–670.

Reid, J. (1987). The learning style preferences of ESL students. *TESOL Quarterly, 21*, 87–111.

Reid, J. M. (Ed.) (1995). *Learning styles in the ESL/EFL classroom*. Boston: Heinle & Heinle.

Renninger, K. A., Hidi, S., & Krapp, A. (Eds.). (1992). *The role of interest in learning and development*. Hillsdale, NJ: Erlbaum.

Rogoff, B. (1994). *Developing understanding of the idea of communities of learners*. Scribner Award Address at the annual meeting of the American Educational Research Association, New Orleans, LA.

Rotter, J. B. (1966). Generalized expectancies for internal versus external control of reinforcement. *Psychological Monographs, 80* (whole no. 609), 1–28.

Rubin, J. (1975). What the "good language learner" can teach us. *TESOL Quarterly, 9*, 41–51.

Samimy, K., & Tabuse, M. (1991). *Situation-specific affective variables in a second language classroom: Analysis and intervention*. Paper presented at the annual meeting of the American Educational Research Association, Chicago, IL.

Saunders, D. (1989). *Type Differentiation Indicator Manual: A scoring system for Form J of the Myers-Briggs Type Indicator*. Palo Alto, CA: Consulting Psychologists Press.

Scarcella, R., & Oxford, R. L. (1992). *The tapestry of language learning: The individual in the communicative classroom*. Boston: Heinle & Heinle.

Schiefele, U. (1991). Interest, learning, and motivation. *Educational Psychologist, 26*, 299–323.

Schmidt, R. (1993). Awareness and second language acquisition. *Annual Review of Applied Linguistics, 13*, 206–226.

Schmidt, R. (1995). Consciousness and foreign language learning: A tutorial on the role of attention and awareness in learning. In R. Schmidt (Ed.), *Attention and awareness in foreign language learning* (Second Language Teaching and Curriculum Center Technical Report No. 9, pp. 1–63). Honolulu: University of Hawai'i, Second Language Teaching & Curriculum Center.

Schmidt, R., & Frota, S. N. (1986). Developing basic conversational ability in a second language: A case study of an adult learner of Portuguese. In R. R. Day (Ed.), *Talking to learn: Conversation in second language acquisition* (pp. 237–325). Rowley, MA: Newbury House.

Schmidt, R., & Savage, W. (1992). Challenge, skill, and motivation. *Pasaa, 22*, 14–28. Reprinted in *University of Hawai'i Working Papers in ESL, 12.2* (1994), 1–25. Honolulu: University of Hawai'i, Department of English as a Second Language.

Schumann, J. H. (1978). The acculturation model for second language acquisition. In R. C. Gingras (Ed.), *Second language acquisition and foreign language teaching* (pp. 27–50). Arlington VA: Center for Applied Linguistics.

Schumann, J. H. (1986). Research on the acculturation model for second language acquisition. *Journal of Multilingual and Multicultural Development, 7*, 379–392.

Schumann, J. H. (1994a). Where is cognition? *Studies in Second Language Acquisition, 16*, 231–242.

Schumann, J. H. (1994b, May). *Stimulus appraisal and second language acquisition.* Paper presented at the conference of the Canadian Association for Applied Linguistics, Vancouver.

Schunk, D. (1991). Self-efficacy and academic motivation. *Educational Psychology, 26*, 207–231.

Scott, W. E. (1976). The effects of extrinsic rewards on "intrinsic motivation." *Organizational Behavior and Human Performance, 15*, 117–129.

Scott, W. E., & Erskine, J. A. (1980). The effects of variations in task design and monetary reinforcers on task behavior. *Organizational Behavior and Human Performance, 25*, 311–335.

Shunk, D. H. (1985). Self-efficacy and classroom learning. *Psychology in the Schools, 22*, 208–223.

Skehan, P. (1989). *Individual differences in second-language learning.* London: Edward Arnold.

Skehan, P. (1991). Individual differences in second-language learning. *Studies in Second Language Acquisition, 13*, 275–298.

Snow, R. E. (1989). Aptitude-treatment interaction as a framework of research in individual differences in learning. In P. L. Ackerman, R. J. Sternberg, & R. Glaser (Eds.), *Learning and individual differences* (pp. 13–59). New York: Freeman.

Snow, R. E., & Swanson, J. (1992). Instructional psychology: Aptitude, adaptation, and assessment. In M. R. Rosenzweig, & L. W. Porter (Eds.), *Annual Review of Psychology, 43*, 583–626.

Steers, R. M., & Porter, L. W. (1975). *Motivation and work behavior*. New York: McGraw-Hill.

Stein, A. H., & Bailey, M. M. (1973). The socialization of achievement motivation in females. *Psychological Bulletin, 80*, 345–366.

Stevick, E. (1995). *Memory, meaning, and method in foreign language learning* (2nd edition). Boston: Heinle & Heinle.

Tessler, M. A., Palmer, M., Farah, T. E., & Ibrahim, B. E. (1987). *The evaluation and application of survey research in the Arab world*. Boulder, CO: Westview Press.

Tharp, R. G., & Gallimore, R. (1988). *Rousing minds to life: Teaching, learning, and schooling in social context*. Cambridge: Cambridge University Press.

Todd, S. (1995). *Questioning questionnaires*. Unpublished paper, University of Hawai'i at Mānoa.

Tomlin, R., & Villa, V. (1994). Attention in cognitive science and second language acquisition. *Studies in Second Language Acquisition, 16*, 183–203.

Tremblay, P. F., & Gardner, R. C. (1995). Expanding the motivation construct in language learning. *Modern Language Journal, 79*, 505–520.

Tucker, R. G., Hamayan, E., & Genesee, F. (1976). Affective, cognitive, and social factors in second language acquisition. *Canadian Modern Language Review 32*, 214–226.

Ur, P. (1984). *Teaching listening comprehension*. Cambridge: Cambridge University Press.

Ushioda, E. (1992, November). *Redefining motivation from the L2 learner's point of view*. Paper presented at IRAAL Conference on Adult Language Learning, Trinity College, Dublin.

Van Patten, B., Lee, J. F., Ballman, T., & Dvorak, T. (1992). *Sabías que...?* New York: McGraw-Hill.

Veroff, J. (1969). Social comparison and the development of achievement motivation. In C. P. Smith (Ed.), *Achievement-related motives in children*. New York: Russell Sage.

Vroom, V. H. (1964). *Work and motivation*. New York: Wiley.

Vygotsky, L. S. (1978). *Mind in society: The development of higher psychological processes*. (M. Cole, V. John-Steiner, S. Scribner, & E. Souberman, Trans., & Eds.). Cambridge, MA: Harvard University Press.

Vygotsky, L. S. (1987). *Collected works*. R. W. Rieber & A. S. Carton (Eds.), N. Minick (Trans.). New York: Plenum.

Wahba, M. A., & Bridwell, L. B. (1976). Maslow reconsidered: A review of research on the need hierarchy. *Organizational Behavior and Human Performance, 15*, 212–240.

Weiner, B. (1972). *Theories of motivation: From mechanism to cognition*. Chicago: Markham.

Weiner, B. (1974). *Achievement motivation and attribution theory*. Morristown, NJ: General Learning Press.

Weiner, B. (1979). A theory of motivation for some classroom experiences. *Journal of Educational Psychology, 71*, 3–25.

Weiner, B. (1985). An attributional theory of achievement motivation and emotion. *Psychological Review, 92*, 548–573.

Weiner, B. (1986). *An attributional theory of motivation and emotion*. New York: Springer-Verlag.

Weiner, B. (1991). Metaphors in motivation and attribution. *American Psychologist, 46*, 921–930.

Wenden, A., & Rubin, J. (Eds.). (1987). *Learner strategies in language learning*. Englewood Cliffs, NJ: Prentice Hall.

Wertsch, J. V. (1985). *Vygotsky and the social formation of mind*. Cambridge: Harvard University Press.

Wesche, M., Edwards, H., & Wells, W. (1982). Foreign language aptitude and intelligence. *Applied Psycholinguistics, 3*, 127–140.

Wong, M. M., & Csikszentmihalyi, M. (1991). Motivation and academic achievement: The effects of personality traits and the quality of experience. *Journal of Personality, 59*, 539–574.

Yager, B. (1991). The constructivist learning model: Towards real reform in science education. *The Science Teacher, 51*, 52–57.

Yang, N-D. (1992). *Second language learners' beliefs about language learning and their use of learning strategies: A study of college students of English in Taiwan*. Unpublished doctoral dissertation, University of Texas at Austin.

Youssef, A. (1984). *Study time, motivation, and students' achievement*. Paper presented at the Annual Meeting of Teachers of English to Speakers of Other Languages, Houston, TX.

ABOUT THE AUTHORS

THE EDITOR

Rebecca Oxford is a professor of language education at the University of Alabama, where she also oversees a department containing 1,700 students. She has written two culture books, as well as several books for language teachers on learning strategies, methodology, and simulation/gaming. Oxford with Robin Scarcella developed the Tapestry Approach, focusing on instruction in the context of motivation, learning styles, and learning strategies. She developed new certification programs in ESL and Japanese and works with Japanese distance education.

THE AUTHORS

Suzuna Abo hails from Japan, where she completed her undergraduate education and worked for several years. She earned an MA in foreign language education from the University of Alabama. She taught Japanese using the "Jorden method" in the Critical Languages Center at the University of Alabama. At this time she is currently teaching Japanese at Hobart and William Smith College in New York State. Her research interests are learning strategies and motivation.

Deena Boraie has a BS in solid state science and an MA in TEFL from the American University in Cairo. She has been the coordinator for testing and research in the Center for Adult and Continuing Education (CACE), the American University in Cairo, and is now head of the Assessment Unit of the CACE. She is a teacher trainer for the Royal Society of Arts Certificate for Overseas Teachers and frequently conducts teacher training workshops in Egypt and Saudi Arabia. She has been involved in motivation research for the last five years.

Zoltán Dörnyei was educated in Eastern Europe and the United States. He did postdoctoral work at the University of California at Los Angeles. He is an associate professor in the Department of Applied Linguistics, Eötvös University, Budapest. His publications include three English language training books, the latest of which, *Conversation and Dialogues in Action*, was published by Prentice Hall in 1992. He publishes widely in major journals in the language instruction field. In the late 1980s he started conducting research that called for changes in conceptions of language learning motivation.

Madeline Ehrman has a PhD in psychology from the Union Institute and degrees in linguistics from Yale University and Brown University. She has worked for many years at the US Foreign Service Institute as a field officer, a language supervisor, and the director of the Research, Evaluation, and Training Group.

She is best known for her work on language learning styles, motivation, and anxiety and has published widely in language learning journals. She is currently writing a book on ways to help language learners who have difficulties (Sage Publications).

Omneya-Karima Fayek Kassabgy has been interested in the topic of foreign language motivation since she wrote her MA thesis in TEFL at the American University in Cairo in 1976 on attitudes and motivation in foreign language learning. She is currently executive vice president of the Career Development Center (CDC), Cairo, where she is responsible for coordinating the educational development division of the center, marketing programs locally and abroad, organizing conferences and seminars, training teachers, and designing a variety of teacher development activities.

Mayumi Okada has returned to Hiroshima, Japan after completing her MA in the Teaching of English to Speakers of Other Languages. She started her research on language learning motivation and strategies while a graduate student in that program. She has taught Japanese to high school students in an award-winning satellite program and has also taught Japanese to university students in Alabama. She has received special training in Japanese instructional methodology at Bryn Mawr College.

Jill Shearin has degrees in French and a doctorate in educational administration. She teaches foreign language education at the University of Alabama and supervises both undergraduate and graduate level teaching interns. She also is the director of the Teacher In-Service Center, which serves large numbers of school districts in the state. Recently she has become a coordinator for the Science in Motion Project, which provides traveling science laboratories to schools throughout the state. She is very interested in what motivates students to learn foreign languages.

Richard Schmidt has taught ESL/EFL and has been a trainer of teachers in Hawai'i, Egypt, Lebanon, and Thailand. Besides his interest in English education, he has a keen interest in the teaching of Arabic and Portuguese as foreign languages. For the past 20 years, he has been at the University of Hawai'i at Mānoa, where he teaches in the MA program in ESL and the PhD program in Second Language Acquisition. He is the director of the National Foreign Language Resource Center at the University of Hawai'i. He has recently explored major issues such as motivation and consciousness in language learning.

SLTCC

TECHNICAL REPORTS

*The Technical Reports of the Second Language Teaching & Curriculum Center
at the University of Hawai'i (SLTCC) report on ongoing curriculum projects,
provide the results of research related to second language learning and teaching,
and also include extensive related bibliographies. SLTCC Technical Reports are
available through University of Hawai'i Press.*

RESEARCH METHODS IN INTERLANGUAGE PRAGMATICS

GABRIELE KASPER
MERETE DAHL

This technical report reviews the methods of data collection employed in 39 studies of interlanguage pragmatics, defined narrowly as the investigation of nonnative speakers' comprehension and production of speech acts, and the acquisition of L2-related speech act knowledge. Data collection instruments are distinguished according to the degree to which they constrain informants' responses, and whether they tap speech act perception/comprehension or production. A main focus of discussion is the validity of different types of data, in particular their adequacy to approximate authentic performance of linguistic action. 51 pp.

(SLTCC Technical Report #1) ISBN 0–8248–1419–3 $10.

A FRAMEWORK FOR TESTING CROSS-CULTURAL PRAGMATICS

THOM HUDSON
EMILY DETMER
J. D. BROWN

This technical report presents a framework for developing methods that assess cross-cultural pragmatic ability. Although the framework has been designed for Japanese and American cross-cultural contrasts, it can serve as a generic approach that can be applied to other language contrasts. The focus is on the variables of social distance, relative power, and the degree of imposition within the speech acts of requests, refusals, and apologies. Evaluation of performance is based on recognition of the speech act, amount of speech, forms or formulæ used, directness, formality, and politeness. 51 pp.

(SLTCC Technical Report #2) ISBN 0–8248–1463–0 $10.

PRAGMATICS OF JAPANESE AS NATIVE AND TARGET LANGUAGE

GABRIELE KASPER
(*Editor*)

This technical report includes three contributions to the study of the pragmatics of Japanese:

- A bibliography on speech act performance, discourse management, and other pragmatic and sociolinguistic features of Japanese;
- A study on introspective methods in examining Japanese learners' performance of refusals;
- A longitudinal investigation of the acquisition of the particle *ne* by nonnative speakers of Japanese.

125 pp.

(SLTCC Technical Report #3) ISBN 0–8248–1462–2 $10.

A BIBLIOGRAPHY OF PEDAGOGY & RESEARCH IN INTERPRETATION & TRANSLATION

ETILVIA ARJONA

This technical report includes four types of bibliographic information on translation and interpretation studies:

- Research efforts across disciplinary boundaries: cognitive psychology, neurolinguistics, psycholinguistics, sociolinguistics, computational linguistics, measurement, aptitude testing, language policy, decision-making, theses, dissertations;
- Training information covering: program design, curriculum studies, instruction, school administration;
- Instruction information detailing: course syllabi, methodology, models, available textbooks;
- Testing information about aptitude, selection, diagnostic tests.

115 pp.

(SLTCC Technical Report #4) ISBN 0–8248–1572–6 $10.

PRAGMATICS OF CHINESE AS NATIVE AND TARGET LANGUAGE

GABRIELE KASPER
(*Editor*)

This technical report includes six contributions to the study of the pragmatics of Mandarin Chinese:

- A report of an interview study conducted with nonnative speakers of Chinese;
- Five data-based studies on the performance of different speech acts by native speakers of Mandarin: requesting, refusing, complaining, giving bad news, disagreeing, and complimenting.

312 pp.

(SLTCC Technical Report #5) ISBN 0–8248–1733–8 $15.

THE ROLE OF PHONOLOGICAL CODING IN READING *KANJI*

SACHIKO MATSUNAGA

In this technical report the author reports the results of a study that she conducted on phonological coding in reading *kanji* using an eye-movement monitor and draws some pedagogical implications. In addition, she reviews current literature on the different schools of thought regarding instruction in reading *kanji* and its role in the teaching of non-alphabetic written languages like Japanese. 64 pp.

(SLTCC Technical Report #6) ISBN 0–8248–1734–6 $10.

DEVELOPING PROTOTYPIC MEASURES OF CROSS-CULTURAL PRAGMATICS

THOM HUDSON
EMILY DETMER
J. D. BROWN

Although the study of cross-cultural pragmatics has gained importance in applied linguistics, there are no standard forms of assessment that might make research comparable across studies and languages. The present volume describes the process through which six forms of cross-cultural assessment were developed for second language learners of English. The models may be used for second language learners of other languages. The six forms of assessment involve two forms each of indirect discourse completion tests, oral language production, and self assessment. The procedures involve the assessment of requests, apologies, and refusals.

(SLTCC Technical Report #7) ISBN 0–8248–1763–X $15.

VIRTUAL CONNECTIONS: ONLINE ACTIVITIES & PROJECTS FOR NETWORKING LANGUAGE LEARNERS

MARK WARSCHAUER
(*Editor*)

Computer networking has created dramatic new possibilities for connecting language learners in a single classroom or across the globe. This collection of activities and projects makes use of e-mail, the World Wide Web, computer conferencing, and other forms of computer-mediated communication for the foreign and second language classroom at any level of instruction. Teachers from around the world submitted the activities compiled in this volume — activities that they have used successfully in their own classrooms.

(SLTCC Technical Report #8) ISBN 0–8248–1793–1 $30.

ATTENTION & AWARENESS IN FOREIGN LANGUAGE LEARNING

RICHARD SCHMIDT
(*Editor*)

Issues related to the role of attention and awareness in learning lie at the heart of many theoretical and practical controversies in the foreign language field. This collection of papers presents research into the learning of Spanish, Japanese, Finnish, Hawaiian, and English as a second language (with additional comments and examples from French, German, and miniature artificial languages) that bear on these crucial questions for foreign language pedagogy.

(SLTCC Technical Report #9) ISBN 0–8248–1794–X $20.

LINGUISTICS AND LANGUAGE TEACHING: PROCEEDINGS OF THE SIXTH JOINT LSH-HATESL CONFERENCE

C. REVES, C. STEELE, C. S. P. WONG
(Editors)

Technical Report #10 contains 18 articles revolving around the following three topics:

- Linguistic issues: These six papers discuss various linguistics issues: ideophones, syllabic nasals, linguistic areas, computation, tonal melody classification, and *wh*-words.

- Sociolinguistics: Sociolinguistic phenomena in Swahili, signing, Hawaiian, and Japanese are discussed in four of the papers.

- Language teaching and learning: These eight papers cover prosodic modification, note taking, planning in oral production, oral testing, language policy, L2 essay organization, access to dative alternation rules, and child noun phrase structure development.

(SLTCC Technical Report #10) ISBN 0–8248–1851–2 $20.

LANGUAGE LEARNING MOTIVATION: PATHWAYS TO THE NEW CENTURY

REBECCA L. OXFORD
(Editor)

This volume chronicles a revolution in our thinking about what makes students want to learn languages and what causes them to persist in that difficult and rewarding adventure. Topics in this book include the internal structures of and external connections with foreign language motivation; exploring adult language learning motivation, self-efficacy, and anxiety; comparing the motivations and learning strategies of students of Japanese and Spanish; and enhancing the theory of language learning motivation from many psychological and social perspectives.

(SLTCC Technical Report #11) ISBN 0–8248–1849–0 $20.

TELECOLLABORATION IN FOREIGN LANGUAGE LEARNING: PROCEEDINGS OF THE HAWAI'I SYMPOSIUM

MARK WARSCHAUER
(Editor)

The Symposium on Local & Global Electronic Networking in Foreign Language Learning & Research, part of the National Foreign Language Resource Center's *1995 Summer Institute on Technology & the Human Factor in Foreign Language Education* included presentations of papers and hands-on workshops conducted by Symposium participants to facilitate the sharing of resources, ideas, and information about all aspects of electronic networking for foreign language teaching and research, including electronic discussion and conferencing, international cultural exchanges, real-time communication and simulations, research and resource retrieval via the Internet, and research using networks. This collection presents a sampling of those presentations.

(SLTCC Technical Report #12) ISBN 0–8248–1867–9 $20.